Mental Health Screening

*How Will It Affect
Your Children?*

Unless otherwise specified, all Scriptures are taken from the King James Version of the Holy Bible.

MENTAL HEALTH SCREENING: HOW WILL IT AFFECT YOUR CHILDREN?
© 2005 by Dennis L. Cuddy

Printed in the United States of America

ISBN 1-933641-01-0

Mental Health Screening

How Will It Affect Your Children?

by Dennis L. Cuddy, Ph.D.

Contents

Foreword

This book is a companion to the earlier work which I wrote, titled *National Mental Health Program: Creating Standards for the New World Order.* That smaller book contained parts 1–4 of a series of articles on mental health, education, and social control. And the impetus for both books has been the recommendation of President George W. Bush's New Freedom Commission on Mental Health that all Americans, and especially children, receive mental health screenings.

In the past, whenever there was controversial congressional legislation regarding children (e.g., funding for comprehensive sex education, allowing privacy-invading questionnaires, etc.), it was easy to introduce and pass provisions in the bills requiring parental consent. However, recent attempts by U.S. Rep. Ron Paul to require parental consent for, and prohibit funding of, mental health screenings failed. This leads many to wonder whether there may be a larger agenda at work here, and it is in parts 5–15 in this new book that this larger agenda, its background, and its future implications, are explored.

Part 5

In April 2002, President George W. Bush established the New Freedom Commission on Mental Health to conduct a "comprehensive study of the United States mental health service delivery system." Now there are about 27 sites around the country piloting various aspects of the president's New Freedom Initiative, which provides for mental health screening for everyone, and provides for strong antipsychotic and antidepressant drugs as treatment for many mental health problems detected.

Perhaps the most powerful force behind this initiative is the pharmaceutical industry, including Eli Lilly & Co. (which manufactures Prozac) whose top selling drug is the antipsychotic Olanzapine. Is it merely a coincidence that President George H. W. Bush has been on the board of directors of Lilly, that Lilly made over $1 million in contributions to George W. Bush and the Republican Party in the campaign of 2000, and that Lilly's CEO, Sidney Taurel, was appointed by the current President Bush to the Homeland Security Council? In July 1945, Lilly chemist Ervin Kleiderer led a research team to an I. G. Farben pharmaceutical plant in Germany. I. G. Farben had produced Zyklon B gas used in the Nazi prison camps (remember that both the Nazis and Communists used mental health screenings to indentify their adversaries). Kleiderer returned to the U.S. with the formula for Dolophine (named in honor of Adolph Hitler), now marketed as methadone. And don't forget that it was Eli Lilly & Co. in 1953 that made up a batch of LSD for the CIA,

according to John Marks in *The Search for the "Manchurian Candidate":
The CIA and Mind Control* (N.Y. Times Books, 1979). Lilly over the years
has given a great deal of money to Planned Parenthood and to the Center
for Population Options.

In case you think you will only be affected by the New Freedom Initiative if you have some extreme form of psychosis or neurosis, you need to
look at whom the leaders in the field consider mentally disturbed. In B. K.
Eakman's "What? Are You Crazy? The Screening of America" (*Chronicles,*
October 2004), she reveals that "in August 2003, the National Institute
of Mental Health and the National Science Foundation announced the
results of their $1.2 million taxpayer-funded study. It stated, essentially,
that traditionalists are mentally disturbed. Scholars from the University
of Maryland, California at Berkeley, and Stanford had determined that
social conservatives, in particular, suffer from 'mental rigidity,' 'dogma-
tism,' and 'uncertainty avoidance,' together with associated indicators of
mental illness."

The ultimate goal of the power elite, as I have written before, is
to have a world government with social control of the populace. In
1919, the American Baptist Publication Society published Samuel
Zane Batten's *The New World Order,* in which he pronounced: "We have
vindicated the right of social control. . . . The state must socialize every
group. . . . Men must learn to have world patriotism. World patriotism
must be a faith." Batten then called for a world federation of nations, and
said that men "must see and affirm that above the nation is humanity.
Internationalism must first be a religion before it can be a reality and a
system."

Because education has been an important vehicle for this movement, a
little over a decade after Batten's book was published, the National Education Association's Department of Superintendence in 1932 published its
Tenth Yearbook subtitled *Character Education.* This document presented
their plans to use America's schools to undermine traditional values in
pursuit of the goal of world government, and see that "the citizen of the
future must be a citizen of the world." (In the companion to this book,
I quoted U.S. Secretary of Education Rod Paige on October 3, 2003 as

saying that he was proud the U.S. was rejoining UNESCO and educating our children to be "citizens of the world." Since "citizens" of states have to obey the states' laws, supposedly "citizens of the world" will have to obey world law. President Clinton also referred to himself as "a citizen of the world" in a speech in Shanghai on July 1, 1998.)

In the companion to this series on mental health, education, and social control, I referred to the head of the Rockefeller Foundation, Max Mason, on April 11, 1933, stating that their goal was social control, the control of human behavior. The next year, in a February 1934 "progress report" by one of the Rockefeller Foundation's division heads, one finds the following: "Can we develop so sound and extensive a genetics that we can hope to breed, in the future, superior men?" (See *The Circuit Riders: Rockefeller Money and the Rise of Modern Science* by Gerald Jones, 1989.) In 1941, the infamous Alfred Kinsey began to receive money for his notorious sex research from Alan Gregg, Rockefeller Foundation medical director, who would also fund the establishment of the Tavistock Institute of Human Relations.

The decade of the 1930s with the Great Depression provided a major impetus for the power elite's goal of social control, and in Bronislaw Malinowski's 1937 conference paper, "Culture as a Determinant Behavior," was mentioned that there was "only one way out" of the current cultural crisis, and that was "the establishment of a scientific control of human affairs." And in that same year, in the July–October 1937 edition of J. L. Moreno's *Sociometry*, one reads about the federal government Resettlement Administration's "Centreville Project," which was an experiment in assigning housing for families based upon certain characteristics (e.g., whether they were religious) to see how they interrelated. President Franklin D. Roosevelt had told Moreno in Hyde Park one day that he would see how Moreno's sociometric principles could be put to use. Perhaps the "Centreville Project" was one such example.

The ultimate goal of the power elite is a world Socialist government, a synthesis of western Capitalism and eastern Communism. A consultant to the Resettlement Administration during this period of the 1930s was Stuart Chase, who in 1932 had authored *A New Deal*, boldly proclaiming:

I am not seriously alarmed by the sufferings of the creditor class, the troubles which the church is bound to encounter, the restrictions of certain kinds of freedom which must result, nor even by the bloodshed of the transition period. A better economic order is worth a little bloodshed. . . . Revolution can give what no other road promises to give so directly and forcibly—a new religion. . . . It will be materialistic. . . . We need a new religion.

With this kind of attitude, one can only wonder why Chase was not only a consultant to the federal Resettlement Administration, but also to UNESCO in 1949. But then perhaps the answer lies in UNESCO's first director-general's emphasis on eugenics. This first director-general, Fabian Socialist Sir Julian Huxley, also advocated a world government, which was perfectly in line with Milton Eisenhower's comment at the closing session of the first day's conference on UNESCO at Wichita, Kansas, December 12, 1947. There, this brother of President Dwight Eisenhower stated that "one can truly understand UNESCO only if one views it in its historical context [and] reviewed in this way it reveals itself as one more step in our halting, painful, but I think very real progress toward a genuine world government." This quote can be found in a speech by U.S. Rep. Paul W. Shafer on March 21, 1952 (later published in his and John Howland Snow's *The Turning of the Tides*).

An ally of Rep. Shafer in Congress was Rep. John Ashbrook, who would severely criticize UNESCO and on October 10, 1962, introduced HR 10508 which would ban psychological testing of students. As support for his legislation, Rep. Ashbrook quoted from a "moral value" exam that had been given to students, asking such things as whether spitting on the Bible or spitting on the flag was worse. Students' values were in the process of being changed, as leading educator Theodore Sizer, writing with his wife in *Five Lectures . . . on Moral Education,* declared in 1970: "Moral autonomy . . . is the 'new morality' toward which we are to guide ourselves and other people. . . . Clearly the strict adherence to a 'code' is out of date." This was a clear example of the humanist influence that was growing in American education (there are 4 million members of the

International Humanist and Ethical Union).

Three years later, the second Humanist Manifesto was written in 1973, and one of its signers was the infamous sexologist Sol Gordon, who referred to himself as "polymorphous perverse." Gordon has been on the board of directors of SIECUS (Sexuality Information and Education Council of the United States), has been affiliated with Ortho Pharmaceuticals (a subsidiary of Johnson & Johnson, which is connected with the Robert Wood Johnson Foundation), has produced the infamous *Zing Sex Comix,* and has called many of those disagreeing with him "Bible Bigots." And in case you think this represents only an isolated extreme example of humanistic attitudes about people who believe in *The Holy Bible,* look at the following quote from a prize-winning essay by John Dunphy in *The Humanist* (January–February 1983): "The battle for humankind's future must be waged and won in the public school classroom . . . between the rotting corpse of Christianity . . . and the new faith of humanism. . . . Humanism will emerge triumphant."

Psychologically, this was all part of a programming process that would culminate in a "brave new world," and how it would be administered was explained in Roderick Seidenberg's 1964 book, *Anatomy of the Future,* in which he showed how a master race of "administrators" controls the masses of human beings "by the ever increasing techniques and refined arts of mental coercion" to the level of mindless guinea pigs.

Similarly, Zbigniew Brzezinski in *Between Two Ages: America's Role in the Technetronic Era* (1970) referred to "the ruling elite" and said that "Society would be dominated by an elite . . . [which] would not hesitate to achieve its political ends by using the latest modern techniques for influencing public behavior and keeping society under close surveillance and control." He also forecast

> difficult problems in determining the legitimate scope of human control. The possibility of extensive chemical mind control, the danger of loss of individuality. . . . Man is increasingly acquiring the capacity to . . . affect through drugs the extent of [children's] intelligence, and to modify and control their personalities.

And he furthered indicated that "in the technetronic society the trend seems to be toward . . . effectively exploiting the latest communication techniques to manipulate emotions and control reason." Mika Brzezinski, one of the people to whom the book was dedicated, is now a correspondent with CBS News.

Along the lines of this same concept that our planet needs to be managed, in 1971 New Age networker Donald Keys co-founded Planetary Citizens (which, in addition to Global Education Associates and others, wants to "redesign education"), and in a later (November 11, 1984) symposium, "Toward a Global Society," stated: "We're at a stage now of pulling it all together. It's a new religion called 'networking.' . . . When it comes to running a world or taking people into a New Age, . . . don't anyone think for a moment that you can run a planet without a head. . . . This planet has to be managed." And Keys is not without influence, as he has been a speechwriter for U.N. Secretary-General U Thant as well as for foreign ministers and ambassadors. In this capacity, he has been responsible for starting many trends at the U.N. Keys has also been with Lucis Trust (formerly Lucifer Publishing), on the board of directors of United World Federalists, and a member of the advisory council of the London Institute of Psychosynthesis. An apparent volunteer for managing people, future governor of California Arnold Schwarzenegger, six years after Keys' 1984 statement, said: "My relationship to power and authority is that I'm all for it. . . . People need somebody to watch over them. . . . Ninety-five percent of the people of the world need to be told what to do and how to behave" (*U.S. News & World Report,* November 26, 1990).

In order to "manage" people, the power elite logically would have to know what we are doing. In that regard, when I was a senior associate with the U.S. Department of Education, one of my jobs was to monitor the federally funded Center for the Social Organization of Schools (CSOS) at Johns Hopkins University. And on December 30, 1985, I wrote a memo to Chester Finn, the head of my division, warning that the CSOS was asking students whether their parents had gotten in trouble with the police, and whether the students themselves would acknowledge being involved in criminal activities.

Also while I was with the U.S. Department of Education, on July 27, 1984, Utah Superintendent of Public Instruction G. Leland Burningham wrote a letter to U.S. Secretary of Education Terrel Bell stating:

> I am forwarding this letter to accompany the proposal which you recommended Bill Spady and I prepare in connection with Outcome-Based Education. This proposal centers around the detailed process by which we will work together to implement Outcome-Based Education using research verified programs. This will make it possible to put Outcome-Based Education in place, not only in Utah but in all schools of the nation.

William Spady is the "father" of Outcome-Based Education (OBE), and he would write in "Future Trends: Considerations in Developing Exit Outcomes" (September 1987) that "Despite the historical trend toward intellectual enlightenment and cultural pluralism, there has been a major rise in religious and political orthodoxy, intolerance, fundamentalism, and conservatism with which young people will have to be prepared to deal." OBE emphasizes the "group" over the individual student, and therefore fits perfectly in the movement toward Socialism. Note the following words of American Communist Party chief Gus Hall: "The battle will be lost, not when freedom of speech is finally taken away, but when Americans become so 'adjusted or conditioned' to getting along with the 'group' that when they finally see the threat, they will say, 'I can't afford to be controversial.'"

Thus, the power elite now apparently believes the public has been conditioned into complacency when forced to submit to such things as mandatory mental health screenings. Alexis De Tocqueville in *Democracy in America* in 1840 warned of this when he explained:

> Above this race of men stands an immense and tutelary power, which takes upon itself alone to secure their gratifications and to watch over their fate. That power is absolute, minute, regular, provident, and mild. It would be like the authority of a parent. . . . It provides for their security,

foresees and supplies their necessities, facilitates their pleasures, manages their principal concerns, directs their industry. . . . After having thus successively taken each member of the community in its powerful grasp and fashioned him at will, the supreme power then extends its arm over the whole community. It covers the surface of society with a network of small complicated rules, minute and uniform. . . . The will of man is not shattered, but softened, bent, and guided. . . . It does not tyrannize, but it compresses, enervates, extinguishes, and stupefies a people, till each nation is reduced to nothing better than a flock of timid and industrious animals, of which the government is the shepherd. . . . It is vain to summon a people who have been rendered so dependent on the central power to choose from time to time the representatives of that power; this rare and brief exercise of their free choice . . . will not prevent them from gradually losing the faculties of thinking, feeling, and acting for themselves, and thus gradually falling below the level of humanity.

Commenting on Illinois' Children's Mental Health Act of 2003, which has flowed from the New Freedom Initiative's initial impetus, Laura Dawn Lewis has described the reasons we all should be concerned. She believes that this act, which requires all children through age eighteen years and all pregnant women to be tested for mental health needs, is wrong because it is profiling, compulsory, a violation of privacy, and unconstitutional.

U.S. Rep. Ron Paul attempted to stop the federal government from mandatory mental health screenings, but he failed. On November 20, 2004, Congress passed the omnibus spending bill without Rep. Paul's amendment, which provided that

> None of the funds made available for the State Incentive Grants for Transformation should be used for any programs of mandatory or universal mental-health screening that performs mental-health screening on anyone under 18 years of age without the express, written permission of the parents or legal guardians of each individual involved.

Kent Snyder, executive director of the Liberty Committee (founded by

Rep. Paul), remarked: "We believe the drug companies and the psychiatric establishment convinced Senators Arlen Specter and Bill Frist to block it." Apparently, the U.S. Senate does not care about parental rights when it comes to something as psychologically invasive as the forced mental health screening of children.

Clearly, the government is seeking more and more power over us, and desires the ability to track us wherever we go. Three days before the *Idaho Statesman* article, WorldNetDaily (WND) on October 7 published "Life With Big Brother: Feds plan to track every car," detailing how the federal Intelligent Transportation Systems Joint Program Office will not only track (using global positioning satellite, GPS, technology) the movement of every vehicle in the nation, but it will also archive this information in massive databases for future use. The first models of vehicles with transceivers, or "onboard units," that will transmit data will be unveiled in 2005, with the goal of equipping 57 million vehicles by 2015. According to the WND article, John Worthington, president and CEO of TransCore (one of the companies currently under contract to develop the onboard units for cars), described the system as "kind of an Orwellian all-singing, all-dancing collector/aggregator/disseminator of transportation information." And three days after the *Idaho Statesman* article, the federal Food and Drug Administration (FDA) on October 13 approved an implantable computer chip containing hospital patients' medical information.

Of course, best of all from the power elite's perspective would be if every American had a national ID card. In that regard, WND on December 8 published "Intel bill to institute national ID system?" which began with the words: "A Republican congressman is decrying the intelligence reform bill set to pass Congress today, saying it creates a de facto national ID-card system. Rep. Ron Paul, R-Texas, says by establishing standards for state drivers' licenses on a federal level, the government is setting up a national system that's 'not proper in a free society'." He further stated that

a national identification card, in whatever form it may take, will allow the federal government to inappropriately monitor the movements and transactions of every American. History shows that governments inevitably use such power in harmful ways. The 9-11 commission, whose recommendations underlie this bill, has called for *internal* screening points where identification will be demanded. Domestic travel restrictions are the hallmark of authoritarian states, not free nations. It is just a matter of time until those who refuse to carry the new licenses will be denied the ability to drive or board an airplane. Nationalizing standards for drivers licenses and birth certificates, and linking them together via a national database, creates a national ID system pure and simple. This legislation imposes federal standards in a federal bill, and it creates a federalized ID regardless of whether the ID itself is still stamped with the name of your state.

Rep. Paul likened an internal checkpoint plan to a "Soviet-style internal passport system."

In the companion to this series on "Mental Health, Education and Social Control," I had mentioned that Ford Foundation president H. Rowan Gaither in the fall of 1953 told the Congressional Reece Committee staff director Norman Dodd:

> Of course, you know that we at the executive level here were, at one time or another, active in either the OSS, the State Department, or the European Economic Administration. During those times, and without exception, we operated under directives issued by the White House. We are continuing to be guided by just such directives. . . . The substance [of these directives] was to the effect that we should make every effort to so alter life in the United States as to make possible a comfortable merger with the Soviet Union.

Fulfilling the power elite's dialectical plan of synthesizing western Capitalism and eastern Communism into a world Socialist government, it clearly looks like we are moving in that direction with more and more government control being exercised over Americans' lives.

Part 6

There are many who believe that recent federal legislation mandates mental health screening of children. However, it does not! Therefore, it seems appropriate at this time to explain what has transpired and why there are concerns.

In February 2001, almost immediately after taking office, President George W. Bush announced his New Freedom Initiative. Then on April 29, 2002, President Bush established the New Freedom Commission on Mental Health (NFCMH), which developed a number of recommendations, among which was mental health screening for Americans, especially children. Then, H.R. 5006 was introduced into the U.S. House of Representatives, and it was later rolled into the larger H.R. 4818, which on December 8, 2004, became Public Law 108-447. In this law, Division F, Title II concerns "Substance Abuse and Mental Health Services," which provides funds for mental health "data collection and evaluation activities." Since it was logical to assume this could include mental health screenings, U.S. Rep. Ron Paul tried to amend the earlier legislation (H.R. 5006) to exclude such screenings, but he was defeated. Later, he tried to amend legislation at least to require parental permission before such screenings would occur. However, he was once again defeated, primarily by U.S. Senate leader Bill Frist and Sen. Arlen Specter. This logically has resulted in the conclusion that Congress indeed does want to allow funds from this public law to be used for mental health screening of children, perhaps even without parental permission. To try to overcome this, Rep. Paul on January 4, 2005, introduced H.R. 181 into the new 109th Congress. The bill is titled "To Prohibit the Use of Federal Funds for Any Universal or Mandatory Mental Health Screening Program" (short title: "Parental Consent Act of 2005").

Although there is no federal law mandating mental health screening, lawyer Phyllis Schlafly in her November 24, 2004, article "No Child Left Unmedicated" has written that "President Bush has instructed 25 federal agencies to develop a plan to implement the NFCMH's recommendations." In her article, she further explained that the NFCMH

> recommends "routine and comprehensive" testing and mental health screening for every child in America, including preschoolers. . . . The NFCMH proposes utilizing electronic medical records for mental health interrogation of both children and adults for mental illnesses in school and during routine physical exams. The NFCMH also recommends integrating electronic health records and personal health information systems. The NFCMH recommends "linkage" of these mental examinations with "state-of-the-art treatments" using "specific medications for specific conditions." . . . "State-of-the-art treatments" will result in many thousands of children being medicated by expensive, ineffective, and dangerous drugs. The long-term safety and effectiveness of psychiatric medications on children have never been proven. The side effects of suggested medications in children are severe. They include suicide, violence, psychosis, cardiac toxicity, and growth suppression. Several school shooters, such as Eric Harris (Columbine) and Kip Kinkel (Oregon) had been on antidepressants or stimulants when they committed their crimes. . . . A Columbia University pilot project of screening students called TeenScreen resulted in one-third being flagged as "positive" for mental health problems, and half of those being turned over for mental health treatment. If this is a preview of what would happen when 52 million public school students are screened, it would mean hanging a libelous label on 17 million American children and putting 8 million children into the hands of the psychiatric/pharmaceutical industry.

And to make it clear that the NFCMH recommendations do not only include children, Dr. Karen Effrem at Phyllis Schlafly's Eagle Forum Conference on September 18, 2004, explained that the NFCMH recommends "screening for mental disorders in primary health care, across the life span, and connect to treatment and supports." Dr. Effrem emphasized, "That is cradle-to-grave."

In part 5 to this series, I mentioned that President Bush had appointed Sidney Taurel, chairman and CEO of Eli Lilly, to the Homeland Security Advisory Council. Eli Lilly & Co. (pharmaceuticals) has manufactured thimerosal, a mercury-based preservative recently removed from childhood vaccines, which has been the subject of recent lawsuits. On November 4, 2002, WRAL television in Raleigh, North Carolina, aired a report stating that "a study sanctioned by the Centers for Disease Control and Prevention shows infants immunized with thimerosal vaccines were 2.5 times more likely to develop neurological disorders, but it was never released (*autismlayer.net*)." And on December 11, 2004, Reuters reporters Maggie Fox and Joanne Kenen wrote that

> members of both the U.S. House of Representatives and Senate vowed to get rid of controversial provisions, slipped quietly into the Homeland Security Act, that they say benefit vaccine makers at the expense of children with autism and other diseases. . . . Tennessee Republican Sen. Bill Frist said the provisions came from a bill he was sponsoring that was aimed at encouraging more companies to make vaccines.

Another drug widely used on children today is Ritalin, which was first marketed by Ciba Company in 1957. According to *The Dan Smoot Report* (August 17, 1970),

> In the 1960s, psychologists discovered that Ritalin works on the central nervous system in children, with a tranquilizing effect. By the late 1960s, Ritalin was being used widely as a personality-changing, mind-controlling drug on small children. . . . [But some] authorities expressed grave concern. Dr. John Dorsey, a Birmingham pediatrician, said: "Here we

are trying . . . to combat increased use of drugs in adolescents, and the schools are recommending that kids be put on this personality-changing drug at the age of five and six." . . . Fritz Redl, professor of behavioral science at Wayne State, said "Ritalin and related drugs are just one more threat in the continuing chemical warfare we are waging on our children."

—See "Drug Is Called Peril to Pupils" by Robert Kraus,
Detroit Free Press, November 7, 1969

More recently, Sean Hannity and Alan Colmes on the Fox News Network (September 26, 2002) interviewed Neil Bush (President Bush's brother) and his son, Pierce. Colmes began by saying,

Neil Bush says too many parents are pressured by educators to give their kids powerful drugs they really don't need. Seven years ago, teachers diagnosed his own son, Pierce, with Attention Deficit Disorder. And doctors prescribed Ritalin to help him concentrate. They later found out Pierce never had ADD.

Pierce Bush said ADD is "way overdiagnosed," and both Neil Bush and Sean Hannity said drugs are "overprescribed" for children. Hannity then commented, "Ritalin acts on the brain the same way cocaine does. And you see now there's a lot of abuse of Ritalin."

Given what Neil and Pierce Bush said, one must wonder why President Bush isn't being more cautious concerning the mental health aspects of his New Freedom Initiative? Perhaps it is because of the influence of communitarianism upon his thinking. In Dana Milbank's February 1, 2001 *Washington Post* article, "Needed: Catchword for Bush Ideology; 'Communitarianism' Finds Favor," one reads:

. . . Some Bush advisors and friends say . . . his actions have less to do with the left vs. the right than with his embrace of many of the ideas contained in the movement known as "communitarianism," which places the importance of society ahead of the unfettered rights of the individual.

"This is the ultimate Third Way," said Don Eberly, an advisor in the Bush White House, using a favorite phrase of President Clinton. . . . Bush's inaugural address, said George Washington University professor Amitai Etzioni, a communitarian thinker, "was a communitarian text." . . . That's no accident: Bush's advisors consulted on the speech with Robert D. Putnam of Harvard University (a leading communitarian thinker). At the same time, Bush has recruited some of the leading thinkers of the "civil society," or "communitarian," movements to his White House. . . . Top Bush strategist Karl Rove introduced Bush to the thinking.

Returning to former FBI agent Dan Smoot, in his *Report* of October 31, 1966, he asked, "When will our water supplies be similarly treated with mind-control drugs to promote mental health?" Smoot further indicated that on August 14, 1965, *Health Bulletin* quoted Dr. Joseph W. Goldzieher, a Texas physician, as saying that governments could control quantity and quality of populations by use of birth-control chemicals, made compulsory upon entire populations "just as salt is iodized or water is fluoridated."

It is worth emphasizing here Dr. Goldzieher's reference to fluoridated water, because prior to its use in water, fluoride had been primarily associated with bug and rat poison. In 1947, President Harry Truman appointed Oscar R. Ewing to head the Federal Security Agency, which included the Public Health Service (later HEW). Ewing hired Edward Bernays (Sigmund Freud's nephew) to develop a propaganda campaign which was successful in getting the American public to accept water fluoridation. Bernays in 1928 had authored *Propaganda,* in which he wrote:

Those who manipulate the organized habits and opinions of the masses constitute an invisible government which is the true ruling power of the country. . . . It remains a fact that in almost every act of our daily lives, whether in the sphere of politics or business, in our social conduct or our ethical thinking, we are dominated by the relatively small number of persons. . . . It is they who pull the wires which control the public mind, who harness old social forces and contrive new ways to bind and guide the world. . . . As civilization has become more complex, and as the need for invisible government has been increasingly demonstrated, the technical means have been invented and developed by which opinion may be regimented.

In case the American public doesn't believe the current Bush administration is capable of using "propaganda," it should be remembered that in early January 2005, it was revealed that the administration had paid commentator Armstrong Williams $240,000 to promote "No Child Left Behind."

By the late 1940s, a "science of coercion" had been developed, and in Colin Simpson's *Science of Coercion: Communication Research and Psychological Warfare 1945-1960,* he refers to

> the engineering of consent of targeted populations at home and abroad.
> . . . Various leaders in the social sciences engaged one another in tacit
> alliances to promote their particular interpretation of society. . . . They
> regarded mass communication as a tool for social management and as a
> weapon in social conflict. . . . Key academic journals of the day . . . con-
> centrated on how modern technology could be used by elites to manage
> social change, extract political concessions, or win purchasing decisions
> from targeted audiences. . . . This orientation reduced the extraordinarily
> complex, inherently communal process of communication to simple
> models based on the dynamics of transmission of persuasive—and, in
> the final analysis,coercive—messages.

Returning to the subject of water fluoridation, what the American public was not told is how the Nazis had used it to control people. In Dr. Swinburne Clymer's *The Age of Treason* (1957), he revealed:

> Charles Eliot Perkins, a research worker in chemistry, biochemistry,
> physiology and pathology, . . . was sent by the United States Government
> to help take charge of the I. G. Farben chemical plants in Germany at
> the end of the Second World War. What follows are statements from
> a letter which Mr. Perkins wrote the Lee Foundation for Nutritional
> Research on October 2, 1954. . . . "In the 1930s Hitler and the German

Nazis envisioned a world to be dominated and controlled by the Nazi philosophy. . . . The German chemists worked out a very ingenious and far-reaching plan of mass control which was submitted to and adopted by the German General Staff. This plan was to control the population in any given area through mass medication of drinking water supplies. By this method they could control the population of whole areas, reduce population by water medication that would produce sterility in the women, and so on. In this scheme of mass control, sodium fluoride occupied a prominent place. . . . The real purpose behind water fluoridation is to reduce the resistance of the masses to domination and control and loss of liberty. . . . There is a small area of the brain tissue that is responsible for the individual's power to resist domination. Repeated doses of infinitesimal amounts of fluorine will in time gradually reduce the individual's power to resist domination by slowly poisoning and narcotizing this area of the brain tissue and make him submissive to the will of those who wish to govern him. . . ."

Not only did the Nazis control populations via water fluoridation, but also through eugenics as well. In *Source Book on European Governments* (1937) by William Rappard, Walter R. Sharp, *et al,* one reads:

A new educational policy has been developed by the Nazis and is now in operation. . . . The terms of an express order issued by the Minister of Education on January 15, 1935 [are] to the effect that courses of instruction in biology shall deal primarily with questions of heredity, . . . mental traits. . . . It is the duty of such institutions to separate the unsuitable and unworthy from those more fitted and capable of advancement and promotion. Constant tests must be made as to physical, moral, mental and general qualifications.

More recently, this eugenic mentality was displayed in the 1996 film, *Extreme Measures* (see the compaion to this book on mental health, education, and social control).

Part 7

It is important to raise questions about what the so-called experts will be doing concerning the mental health screenings recommended by the New Freedom Commission on Mental Health (NFCMH). Some of these questions have been raised by Dr. Jane Orient (executive director of the Association of American Physicians and Surgeons) in her article, "Are Your Children Crazy?" She has asked among many other questions, what are the credentials of the screeners, what are the criteria for possible abnormality, what is the scientific validation, will you be allowed to get a second opinion, can you see the record and enter corrections if indicated, what will happen if your child fails the screen, what sort of treatment will be given, who will supervise it, what if you don't approve of it, can you refuse to participate in the program, and what are the repercussions if you refuse to participate?

In case you don't think you have to raise these questions because you haven't heard anything about the NFCMH recommendations being implemented in your state, think again! On January 21, 2005, Leslie La-Prise (information center manager for the Substance Abuse and Mental Health Services Administration of the federal Department of Health and Human Services) sent an e-mail stating that "all the states are moving toward implementation of the New Freedom Commission report."

In terms of the elite's social control of the populace, what happens to those who resist mental health screenings and the labeling that may ensue is important, given what Erich Fromm wrote in the afterword of the commemorative edition of George Orwell's book *1984*. Fromm explains that "Orwell shows quite clearly that in a system in which the concept of truth as an objective judgment concerning reality is abolished, anyone who is a minority of one must be convinced he is insane." Judgments made from mental health screenings as to whether one is "abnormal" will often be subjective rather than representative of objective "truth." If you complain about such screenings, there may be an attempt to isolate you as someone who overreacts. Have you ever heard of parents who went to school about a problem there, only to be told they are the only ones to have complained, even though the "truth" is that other parents have expressed concern about the same problem?

Also, if government officials tell you it is the "truth" that the medical records from mental health screenings will be kept confidential, will we be able to believe them? Not hardly! *The Health Freedom Watch* (November/December 2004) reported that on November 15, 2004, the U.S. Department of Health and Human Services (HHS) called for public comments on its plans for a National Health Information Network (NHIN). This would include establishing "interoperable" (easily exchanged) electronic health records for all citizens. One of the main purposes of the network is to "improve advanced bio-surveillance methods." But the effect of the NHIN would be to eliminate individuals' freedom to give or withhold their consent before their health information is released to others.

The goal of the power elite is eventually to be able to track the activities of everyone, and maintain detailed files on them. In this regard, it is worth remembering what Edward Cornish, the president of the World Future Society, said about this. In Jon Van's May 7, 1996, article in the *Chicago Tribune* about microchips implanted under the skin, one reads:

> Inevitably, implantable radio locators conjure up visions of Big Brother and unscrupulous scientists abusing such technology to control the masses. . . . Edward Cornish (president of the World Future Society) believes, at least initially, that such chips would be voluntary. But he

acknowledges that "things that are voluntary today have a way of becoming compulsory tomorrow."

In *Friendly Fascism: The New Face of Power in America* by Bertram Gross (who helped draft major social legislation during the years of presidents Roosevelt and Truman), there is a section titled "Womb-to-Tomb Dossiers," in which one reads about

> the new statistical data banks being set up in the fields of education, health, and mental health. . . . As of early 1980 detailed plans were worked out to register the country's young people without their knowing through what is known as "passive" or "faceless" registration. This would be done by compiling a computerized list of names and addresses by assembling the information from school records, the Internal Revenue Service, the Social Security systems, and state driver's license bureaus. . . . With the growth of a computerized dossier network, and enough R&D investment in its perfection, it will be possible to keep up-to-date inventories on all employees in America. . . . Outcries against misinformation in files could be met by procedures for providing fuller information. . . . The central thrust of those demanding protection of individual rights to privacy and due process could be deflected by developing complicated devices for the purging or destruction of incriminating files—devices that the oligarchs themselves could easily utilize for their own protection and that of their most trustworthy managerial and technical aides.

In Gross' book, there is also a section titled "A Good Neighbor in a New World Order," and in terms of what to look for, Gross warns:

> Anyone looking for black shirts, mass parties or men on horseback will miss the telltale clues of this creeping fascism. . . . In America, it would be supermodern and multi-ethnic—as American as Madison Avenue, executive luncheons, credit cards and apple pie. It would be fascism with a smile. . . . One can look forward to improved capabilities . . . for the use of induced heart failure . . . induced suicide . . . and "accidental" automobile fatalities.

Of course, the government will offer a good reason for having to track everyone, such as the need to avoid future terrorist attacks. Recently, Congress passed a new homeland security measure that requires the federal government to work with states over the next eighteen months to devise security standards for identification cards and drivers' licenses. In Ledyard King's Gannett News Service article on December 30, 2004, about this, he related that

> Marv Johnson, a lawyer with the Washington office of the American Civil Liberties Union, said the IDs created under the new law won't make the country any safer. Most countries experiencing a high rate of terrorism have a national ID, and one-third of those use biometric identifiers, according to the ACLU. The new licenses will give the federal government another way to keep track of citizens while creating a false sense of security, Johnson said. "You're not going to stop counterfeiting and you're not going to stop forgeries," he said. "It will cost more, [but] it will be much easier to steal someone's identity."

In addition to using drivers' licenses as national IDs, there is within the Department of Transportation the Intelligent Transportation Systems Joint Program Office, which is coordinating a plan to track every American driver. According to a "Vision Statement" published by the Federal Highway Administration in 2003, each private "travel customer" by 2022 will have her or his own "user profile" stored in databases.

The federal government is already developing identification card standards for all federal employees, including military personnel. It is called the Personal Identity Verification Project and is the result of an August 27, 2004, presidential directive. It is managed by the Commerce Department's National Institute of Standards and Technology, and could cause private businesses to develop similar standards for identifying (and tracking) employees.

If the public begins to resist these efforts to monitor their activities, there will probably be a crisis (manufactured or not) which will induce the populace to abandon their resistance. Tavistock senior fellow Fred

Emery in *Futures We Are In* notes that he developed a theory of "social turbulence," which explains that many individuals faced with a series of crises will attempt to reduce the tension and stress by adaptation and eventually psychological retreat (similar to Pavlov's protective inhibition response). Thus, what will happen with an upcoming crisis will be similar to what Crassus did during the days of the Roman Empire when he used Spartacus' rebellion to cause Romans to give up some of their rights in their republic in order to be secure by giving Crassus more power.

Today, we have already given up some of our freedoms under the Patriot Act (2001) and Homeland Security Act (2002), supposedly in order to protect us from terrorists. But remember that famous author C. S. Lewis warned that "of all tyrannies, the tyranny sincerely exercised for the good of its victim may be the most oppressive." Do you recall when Attorney-General John Ashcroft said the Patriot Act and Homeland Security Act would only be applied to terrorists, so the average American had nothing to worry about? Well, recently an average American was star-gazing with his daughter, pointed a laser beam at an aircraft while doing this, and is now charged with violating the Homeland Security Act.

In President George W. Bush's second inaugural address on January 20, 2005, he said "we have lit . . . a fire in the minds of men." But why would he say this, given that the phrase "fire in the minds of men" comes from Fedor Dostoevski's *The Possessed* (later published as *The Devils*), and Dostoevski wrote an 1873 essay explaining:

> In my novel *The Possessed*, I made the attempt to depict the manifold and heterogeneous motives which may prompt even the purest of heart and the most naive people to take part in the perpetration of so monstrous a villainy. The horror lies precisely in the fact that in our midst the filthiest and most villainous act may be committed by one who is not a villain at all! This, however, happens not only in our midst but throughout the world; it has been so from time immemorial, during transitional epochs, at times of violent commotion in people's lives—doubts, negations, scepticism and vacillation regarding the fundamental social convictions. But in our midst this is more possible than anywhere else, and

precisely in our day; this is the most pathological and saddest trait of our present time—the possibility of considering oneself not as a villain, and sometimes almost not being one, while perpetrating a patent and incontestable villainy—therein is our present-day calamity!

Is this revealing about the hubris being exhibited by some top government officials today?

The power elite, which wants to exercise social control over us, plans far in advance. According to Holly Swanson, author of *Set Up and Sold Out*, she received copies of the incorporation documents for the Gorbachev Foundation at the Presidio from the California Department of State, and found they were filed six months *before* the so-called collapse of the Soviet Union and Mikhail Gorbachev's resignation as president of the USSR on December 26, 1991. Just before the Gorbachev Foundation's first State of the World Forum (September 27–October 1, 1995), the *Washington Post* published "Global Chic: Gorby's Bash by the Bay" (September 24, 1995) by George Cothran, who wrote that "maybe challenging the powers-that-be isn't Gorbachev's main objective. Rather than disrupting the hide-bound elites that run the world, the former Soviet president seems more intent on rejoining their exclusive club."

From where did the concept of an elite exercising social control over the masses of people come? About six hundred years before the birth of Jesus Christ, the priests at the temple of Isis in Sais, Egypt, told the Greek philosopher Solon about Atlantis, and that only the Aryans survived its destruction. They indicated that the Aryans resided at Shamballa and used the power of the "sun wheel," called the swastika (swastikas have reportedly been found in the vault of the Yale University secret society called Skull & Bones). About two hundred years after Solon was told about Atlantis, Plato picked up the story of Atlantis and the Aryans. And in his book, *The Republic,* he described a plan whereby the people would be ruled by an elite. Closer to our own time, Sir Francis Bacon wrote *The New Atlantis,* which he considered to be America. Then, in the mid-1800s, John Ruskin (who has a swastika on his grave) read Plato every day, and became the mentor of Cecil Rhodes (and Gandhi). There were Ruskin colonies in Tennessee and Georgia from 1894 to 1901 (see W. Fitzhugh Brundage's *A Socialist Utopia in the New South*). Rhodes in 1891 formed a secret society, "The Society of the Elect," to "take the government of the whole world," in Rhodes' own words. The famous author Rudyard Kipling (who has swastikas on many of his books) became a member of the Rhodes Trust, and in 1902 wrote a letter to the famous Fabian Socialist author H. G. Wells concerning the latter's new book, *Anticipations* (1901). (I have obtained a copy of this letter, and it is reprinted here.)

In *Anticipations,* Wells wrote about a New Republic (just as Bacon had written about a New Atlantis), and said "the men of the new republic . . . will have an ideal that will make killing worth the while." Wells renamed the New Republic to the "New World Order," which was the title of his 1939 book, in which he stated: "In the great struggle to evoke a Westernized World Socialism, contemporary governments may vanish. . . . Countless people . . . will hate the new world order . . . and will die protesting against it." Given what Wells said, why would President George H. W. Bush in 1990 adopt the term "new world order" for his vision for the world?

At the first State of the World Forum hosted by the Gorbachev Foundation mentioned above, speaker Sam Keen evoked loud applause when he remarked, "If we cut the world's population by 90 percent, there won't be enough people left to do ecological damage." Think what it would take to reduce the world's population by 90 percent! Wouldn't it be unconscionable for a moral society to just stand by while Sam Keen or any other population controllers carry out their plans?

Part 8

The role of elite corporations and foundations in promoting social control over the masses via the mental health and mental hygiene movements cannot be overestimated. James McKeen Cattell was president of the Psychological Corporation (founded in 1921), and he wrote that "whatever the people have thought over the years that the various Carnegie organizations were contributing to education, their mission, as stated, has been 'to promote the extension of applied psychology'." William James (father of American psychology) founded the National Committee for Mental Hygiene, and according to B. K. Eakman in *Cloning of the American Mind: Eradicating Morality Through Education,* he

> persuaded Rockefeller to contribute millions to the National Committee for Mental Hygiene. . . . The goal of the Committee was specifically to prevent mental illness, and its focus was elementary and secondary schools. The thrust of the Committee's philosophy was that mental illness hinged on faulty personality development in childhood and that, therefore, personality development should supersede all other educational objectives. Stress was seen as the chief culprit, and parents and other authority figures as the second. This anti-stress wisdom was echoed by the 1930 White House Conference on Child Health and Protection, which predictably revolved around a group of humanistic psychologists from Teachers College (Columbia University)."

John Dewey (father of progressive education) led these psychologists, and he co-authored the first Humanist Manifesto in 1933. These humanistic psychologists believed society's values needed to be changed, but there would be resistance. In the official statement released by the International Congress on Mental Health, held in London in 1948, one finds:

> The social sciences and psychiatry also offer a better understanding of the great obstacles to rapid progress in human affairs. Man and his society are closely interdependent. Social institutions such as family and school impose their imprint early in the personality development of their members, who in turn tend to perpetuate the traditional pattern to which they have been moulded. It is the men and women in whom these patterns of attitude and behavior have been incorporated who present the immediate resistance to social, economic and political changes."

The change Dewey and his fellow progressive educators wanted was toward Socialism (he was with the Intercollegiate Socialist Society which later became the League for Industrial Democracy), which emphasizes the group over the individual. However, in Vice-Admiral H. G. Rickover's *Education and Freedom* (1959), he explained that "our educational leaders have never received a clear mandate from the American people to follow the theories of John Dewey and his disciples. We have never authorized them to change the objectives of formal education from teaching basic subjects to conditioning children for group life." Rickover indicated that under the Soviet educational system of that time, "education was to be replaced by training; development of young minds by behavioral conditioning." Doesn't this sound like what is happening in America today under school-to-work and values clarification?

By the 1960s, the progressive education philosophy of Teachers' College permeated the American public schools and there was a shift in emphasis from the cognitive (academic basics) to the affective (social relationships and feelings) domain. This marked the beginning of rampant grade inflation and social promotions which, it was believed, would reduce students' "stress." Also, it would be easier to exercise social control (manipulate) over people conditioned to emphasize "feelings" over "thinking."

After the shift to "feelings" had occurred, the journal *Mental Hygiene* (which changed its name to *M.H.* in the early 1970s) had a new aim. According to Walter Bromberg in *From Shaman to Psychotherapist*, this new aim was "to involve the 'growing number of citizens faced with major policy decisions' in public situations that affect mental health. These can be population control, abortions, ecology, civil rights, pollution, and social planning of many descriptions."

In the next decade, the president of the History of Education Society, Sol Cohen, delivered a speech in 1982 revealing the influence which the mental hygiene movement had on education. The speech was titled, "The Mental Hygiene Movement, the Development of Personality and the School: The Medicalization of American Education" (*History of Education Quarterly,* Summer 1983), and in it, Cohen related that "few intellectual and social movements of this century have had so deep and pervasive an influence on the theory and practice of American education as the mental hygiene movement."

Two years after Cohen delivered his speech, the U.S. Department of Education received testimony from around the nation regarding proposed regulations to implement "The Protection of Pupil Rights Amendment." Phyllis Schlafly published the testimony in *Child Abuse in the Classroom* (1984), and three examples are pertinent to the subject of mental health. Cris Shardelman of the state of Washington explained that

> under the guise of Mental Health, a program called WOW was developed at the Northwest Regional Laboratory. This program would have had the primary children exploring their attitudes, beliefs and values concerning such things as double standards, sexual exploitation, guilt and embarrassment about sexual activity, masturbation, homosexuality, and recognition of such words as stud and prostitute. . . . I believe that at least one suicide was the result of the implementation of the suicide section of the mental health program.

Rev. Ronald Wilson of Oregon testified:

My son is scheduled to be instructed in the ideal age to start having sexual intercourse when he takes grade 8. In Mental Health next year, he will be required to complete the sentence: "In my value system the ideal age to start having sexual intercourse is _____." Age is not the question in the traditional moral Christian system—marriage is the criterion. By leading the student to assume that age is the criterion, atheistic humanism is being taught.

And Lawrence Dunegan, M.D., of Pennsylvania related that

in our high school recently, in what was called a Health class, 11th grade students were given a series of questions for each of which they were to choose one of two possible answers. They were then told to grade their own papers on a point system according to which answer was given. They were then told that this was a mental health index. They were told right there in the classroom that anybody scoring above a certain number of points had a serious mental health problem and was in need of psychiatric care. At that point, one girl burst into tears right in the middle of her classroom.

Dr. Dunegan also indicated that a severe emotional impact was sustained even several days after the questions were presented, and that "those who prepare this kind of material for use in the schools are insensitive to the damage they are doing."

For the elite, human life is not something precious that should be preserved. Human beings are to be bred and managed just like any other useful animal. This is why a leading Fabian Socialist like Harold Laski could write a letter on May 7, 1927, to U.S. Supreme Court Justice Oliver Wendell Holmes (who had just written the eugenic *Buck v. Bell* decision) saying, "Sterilize all the unfit, among whom I include all fundamentalists." In *The Final Days* by Bob Woodward and Carl Bernstein, they wrote that "in [Gen. Alexander] Haig's presence, [Henry] Kissinger referred pointedly to military men as 'dumb, stupid animals to be used' as pawns for foreign policy." Someone might say at this point that while this is a horrible attitude regarding our servicemen and servicewomen, surely our government would not treat them as animals. Think again! Our government actually has treated military service personnel like laboratory animals.

In an editorial, "Chemical Vets: Disgraceful treatment of a special WWII group" (November 11, 2004), in the *Detroit Free Press,* one discovers that an estimated seventy thousand American troops were used in some form of chemical experimentation during World War II. The editorial also states that

> the men of the Army's 1st Chemical Casual Company were deceived into becoming guinea pigs for inhumane tests of chemical weapons and protective gear during World War II, kept in the dark about the potential consequences of their exposure, denied redress for injuries inflicted on them by their government, and then, as they advanced in years, cruelly promised help that has yet to arrive. This is a shameful situation. . . .

And for those who believe President Bush really cares about the soldiers he has sent to fight and die in Iraq, why don't you ask him why he has just proposed cutting the Veterans Administration 2005 budget request by $1.2 billion over the objections of the Secretary of Veterans Affairs!

How can our government say we have to go to war to bring freedom to people in other countries when there's a war going on in this country to deprive our children of freedom from government intervention and coercion (e.g., mental health screenings, requiring psychotropic drugs, privacy-invading questionnaires, values-altering teaching techniques, etc.)? U.S. Rep. Ron Paul in his February 7, 2005, speech, "What does Freedom Really Mean?" (*www.house.gov/paul/tst/tst2005/tst020705.htm*), explained:

> Simply put, freedom is the absence of government coercion. . . . "Liberalism," which once stood for civil, political, and economic liberties, has become a synonym for omnipotent coercive government. . . . "Conservatism," which once meant respect for tradition and distrust of active government, has transformed into big-government utopian grandiosity.

And Rep. Paul then reminded us of President Ronald Reagan's warning: "Man is not free unless government is limited. There's a clear cause and effect here that is as neat and predictable as a law of physics: As government expands, liberty contracts."

Who exactly does the federal government consider someone with a mental health problem? According to the June 1998 *Federal Register*, the prevalence rate for children with "serious emotional disturbance" (SED) is 10–12 percent. And what is a seriously emotionally disturbed child? According to at least one state's mental health plan, he or she can be a "child, under the age of 18, with atypical development (up to age 5)." With this broad definition, no wonder they say 10–12 percent of the child population has SED !

In an effort to block the current federal initiative regarding mandatory mental health screenings of children, U.S. Rep. Ron Paul has introduced H.R. 181 "Parental Consent Act of 2005." And in his January 31, 2005, speech, "Don't Let Congress Fund Orwellian Psychiatric Screening of Kids" (*www.house.gov/paul/tst/tst2005/tst013105.htm*), Rep. Paul states:

> Every parent in America should be made aware of a presidential initiative called the "New Freedom Commission on Mental Health." This commission issued a report last year calling for the mandatory mental health screening of American schoolchildren, meaning millions of kids will be forced to undergo psychiatric screening whether their parents consent or not.
>
> At issue is the fundamental right of parents to decide what medical treatment is appropriate for their children. Forced mental health screening simply has no place in a free or decent society. The government does not own you or your kids, and it has no legitimate authority to interfere in your family's intimate health matters. . . . It is important to understand that powerful interests, namely federal bureaucrats and pharmaceutical lobbies, are behind the push for mental health screening in schools.
>
> There is no end to the bureaucratic appetite to run our lives, and the pharmaceutical industry is eager to sell psychotropic drugs to millions of new customers in American schools. . . . Refer to my congressional

website for articles from September 2004 about mental health screening, and sobering statistics about antidepressant drugs and kids in the text of H.R. 181. Most of all, talk with your friends, family, and colleagues about the underlying issue of whether the state owns your kids. Remind them that freedom can be maintained only when state power is limited, especially when it comes to fundamental freedoms over our bodies and minds.

And for those who believe the government really cares about our mental health, why do government officials annually recommend that especially older people receive flu shots? Aren't they aware that H. Hugh Fudenberg, M.D. (vice-president and director of Research, Neuroimmuno Therapeutics Research Foundation) has indicated that clinically normal individuals aged 60–65 who receive influenza vaccine three or four times during a five-year period will five years later have an incidence of Alzheimer's disease ten-fold greater than aged matched individuals who did not receive it?

Not only are there questions about the effects of flu shots upon mental health, but there are also questions about the effects of antidepressants upon our mental health. Concerning programs such as TeenScreen (a suicide questionnaire program), Marcia Angell (a medical ethics lecturer at Harvard Medical School and author of *The Truth About Drug Companies*) said, "It's just a way to put more people on prescription drugs" and that such programs would boost the sale of antidepressants like Paxil, Zoloft, and Prozac even after the FDA last September ordered warning labels on the drugs saying they might be the cause of suicidal thoughts or actions by minors. This information comes from Hans Eisenman of PR WEB (727-452-5241), who also points out that the originator of TeenScreen, David Shaffer, is a "paid consultant to more than one pharmaceutical company, including GlaxoSmithKline, maker of antidepression drugs, Paxil and Seroxat.

Part 9

The power elite are increasingly encroaching upon our inalienable rights and liberties, and the future they have planned for us was described in *Our Benevolent Feudalism* (1902) by W. J. Ghent (former editor of *The American Fabian*). Famous author Jack London in *The Iron Heel* (1907) referred to Ghent's book as "the textbook" the "oligarchs" will use to rule the future. London said the oligarchs and plutocrats will have new ways "of moulding the thought processes of the nation." In his book, Ghent wrote regarding the people that "all their old liberties were gone. . . . Likewise was denied them . . . the right to bear or possess arms. . . . They were machine serfs and labor serfs." More recently, Dr. Stan Monteith of Radio Liberty said his good friend Congressman William Dannemeyer told him that David Rockefeller had informed Dannemeyer: "There are some men born to rule. Most men are born to be ruled."

Of course, the public has to be prepared to accept willingly control by the power elite. One means of accomplishing this is for the public to be convinced they are in need of the benevolent help of certain authority figures such as health professionals. It is not wise, though, automatically to accept what they say as advantageous to our health. For example, in an earlier part of this series, I referred to the dangers of the mercury-based preservative thimerosal, which has been given in vaccines to young children by doctors across this land. At about the same time the Environmental Protection Agency (EPA) was warning the public about the small amount of mercury in certain fish, U.S. Rep. Dan Burton discovered that his previously normal, but now autistic, grandchild had been given vaccines in one day with forty times the amount of mercury considered safe by the EPA! And this has happened to numerous children across the U.S., while the rate of autism has dramatically increased.

Among the health professionals whose benevolent help the public is to be convinced they need are those in the field of mental health. However, it should be asked to what extent government supported mental health programs actually contribute to the mental health problems they are supposed to remedy. For example, North Carolina published *Life Skills for Health: Focus on Mental Health 10-12*, which contains as a health education resource "A Newspoem" from *The New York Times* (February 7, 1968) that has a girl deliberately shooting herself in the head when her parents tell her to shoot her dog. Isn't it possible that some students might actually develop mental health problems, or exacerbate existing mental health problems, by reading such assignments? The North Carolina *Life Skills for Health: Focus on Mental Health* has been distributed by the National Humanistic Education Center (renamed Sagamore Institute in 1980) in New York.

Additional educational activities that can negatively impact students' mental health have included teaching elementary school students the theme song from "M*A*S*H" (which is actually titled "Suicide Is Painless") and "death education." An educational regent from New York called me and said she remembered a national television special several years ago where a student at Columbine High School in Colorado said she had thought about suicide after taking death education.

One way mental health professionals have tried to convince the people that they are in need of help is to broaden the definition of what are considered mental health problems. In part 8 of this series, I referred to TeenScreen, a program screening ninth and tenth graders in thirty-six states for risk of suicide, anxiety disorders, depression, and drug and alcohol disorders. According to the February 2005 *Education Reporter,* "TeenScreen officials say that generally up to one-third of the students who undergo screening show some signs of mental health problems, and about half of those are referred to mental health services—for a total of about 15 percent of the students screened." A typical question from Teen-Screen is "Have you often felt very nervous when you've had things to do in front of people?" If this is supposed to be an indication of someone having a mental health problem, then who doesn't have one? As you can see, these types of questions can additionally be considered an invasion of one's right to privacy.

But the breadth of who should be covered by mental health services is even greater than those who feel nervous doing things in front of people. According to the president's New Freedom Commission Report of 2002 (and the Surgeon General's Report of 1999), services for children and their families should be based upon outcomes that demonstrate

> achievement of expected developmental cognitive, social, and emotional milestones and by secure attachments, satisfying social relationships, and effective coping skills. Mentally healthy children and adolescents enjoy a positive quality of life, meet developmental milestones, function well at home, in school, and in their communities; and are free of disabling symptoms of psychopathology.
>
> —Kimberly Hoagwood et al., 1996

As mentioned in part 8 of this series, the New Freedom Commission on Mental Health has recommended the mandatory mental health screening of American schoolchildren. However, on January 4, 2005, U.S. Rep. Ron Paul introduced H.R.181, the "Parental Consent Act of 2005" in an effort to block this mandatory screening. By early March 2005, Rep. Paul had twenty-six co-sponsors for his legislation. They are: U.S. Reps. Akin, Bartlett, Calvert, Camp, Davis, Everett, Feeney, Foxx, Garrett, Goode, Gutknecht, Hunter, Hyde, Jones, Mark Kennedy, Manzullo, McCotter, Jeff Miller, Neugebauer, Norwood, Otter, Pence, Rogers, Simpson, Tancredo and Wamp.

Usually, broad governmental interventions into the home and school are associated with Democrats. For example, Democrat former governor James B. Hunt, Jr. (mentioned in an earlier part of this series) in the late 1970s had a long-range plan of pulling together from departments of education and human resources a variety of screening, rehabilitative, and training services into a public school kindergarten program beginning at age 2 "for those most in need." He, Hillary Clinton, and others a decade later as part of the National Center on Education and the Economy went even further and developed a "cradle-to-grave" system of "human resource development." But this interventionist attitude is not exclusively the domain of Democrats, as the New Freedom Initiative belongs to President George W. Bush, a Republican. And Republican U.S. Senator Lamar Alexander, when he was U.S. Secretary of Education over a dozen years ago, believed the new American school should be open year round from 6:00 a.m. to 6:00 p.m., and he said that

> those schools will serve children from age 3 months old to 18 years. That may be shocking to you, but if you were to do an inventory of every baby in your community, and think about what the needs of those babies were for the next four or five years, you might see that those needs might not be served in any other way.

The encroachment upon our rights and liberties today also comes through such things as the Homeland Security Act and the Patriot Act. We are told such Acts are necessary because we are in a war against terrorism. However, we should remember what U.S. Supreme Court Justice David Davis said in *Ex Parte Milligan, 4 Wallace 2* (1866):

> The Constitution of the United States is a law for rulers and people, equally in war and peace and covers with the shield of its protection all classes of men, at all times, and under all circumstances. No doctrine, involving more pernicious consequences, was ever invented by the wit of man than that any of its provisions can be suspended during any of the great exigencies of government. Such a doctrine leads directly to anarchy or despotism, but the theory of necessity upon which it is based is false, for the Government, within the Constitution, has all the powers granted to it, which are necessary to preserve its existence; as has been happily proved by the result of the great effort to throw off its just authority.

Besides, do you really feel more secure with the Department of Homeland Security (DHS)? On February 15, 2005, the U.S. Senate by a vote of 98–0 approved Michael Chertoff as the new secretary of DHS. He's the one who, when head of the FBI's Criminal Division, said after the terrorists' attack of 9/11: "We're not interested in talking with Special Agent [Robert] Wright." FBI Special Agent Wright had been following terrorists' money laundering via various Islamic "charities" in the U.S. before 9/11, and on June 9, 2001 (three months *before* 9-11) warned of future terrorist attacks against American interests and the needless loss of American lives. But the new secretary of DHS had no interest in even talking to Special Agent Wright, and the U.S. Senate approved Chertoff anyway! This is reminiscent of the Senate approving Strobe Talbott as President Clinton's deputy secretary of state by a similarly overwhelming margin even *after* Talbott had written in *Time* (July 20, 1992) that "perhaps national sovereignty wasn't such a great idea after all" and "the case for world government" was "clinched."

For the power elite to control us, it is first necessary for them to track us. Matt Richtel in *The New York Times* (November 17, 2004) reported that "Spring Independent School District in Texas is equipping 28,000 students with ID badges containing computer chips that are read when students get on and off school buses." And in a separate story, on January 18, 2005, Principal Earnie Graham of Brittan Elementary School in Sutter, California, without parental input began requiring students to wear radio frequency ID badges that can track each student's every move. According to Associated Press writer Lisa Leff (*Houston Chronicle,* February 10, 2005), Graham hopes to add bar codes to the IDs, so that students can also use them to pay for cafeteria meals and to check out library books. Graham, who is also school superintendent, "told objecting parents that their children could be disciplined for boycotting the badges." A few days after this article appeared, the company that developed this technology pulled out of the agreement with the school and Superintendent Graham expressed his disappointment with their decision.

The best way for the power elite to monitor our activities would be for everyone to have a national ID, and on February 10, 2005, the U.S.

House of Representatives passed H.R. 418 by a vote of 261–161 specifying requirements for each state's drivers' licenses and personal identification cards to be recognized by any federal agency. The requirements include "minimum data elements" with "electronic storage in a transferable format" conducive to "sharing of driver license data." In other words, a national ID !

But perhaps just as troubling as the national ID is Section 102 of H.R. 418 which states: "Notwithstanding any other provision of law, the Secretary of Homeland Security shall have the authority to waive, and shall waive, all laws such Secretary, in such Secretary's sole discretion, determines necessary to ensure expeditious construction of the barriers and roads under this section." The section also says there will be no judicial review! Jeff Deist, a spokesman for U.S. Rep. Ron Paul, asked if "all laws" would include the Posse Comitatus Act (which prohibits the use of the military to execute the laws of the United States except where expressly authorized by Congress)? Do you really want Michael Chertoff waiving "all laws" that at his "sole discretion" he "determines necessary" to waive?

Regarding H.R. 418, U.S. Rep. Ron Paul in his February 14, 2005, weekly column, titled "The National ID Trojan Horse," revealed that

Supporters claim the national ID scheme is voluntary. However, any state that opts out will automatically make non-persons out of its citizens. The citizens of that state will be unable to have any dealings with the federal government because their ID will not be accepted. They will not be able to fly or to take a train. In essence, in the eyes of the federal government they will cease to exist. It is absurd to call this voluntary, and the proponents of the national ID know that every state will have no choice but to comply. Federal legislation that nationalizes standards for drivers' licenses and birth certificates creates a national ID system pure and simple. It is just a matter of time until those who refuse to carry the new licenses will be denied the ability to drive or board an airplane. Such domestic travel restrictions are the hallmark of authoritarian states, not free republics.

This bill establishes a huge, centrally-coordinated database of highly personal information about American citizens. . . . The bill even provides for this sensitive information of American citizens to be shared with Canada and Mexico! Imagine a corrupt Mexican official selling thousands of identity files, including Social Security numbers, to criminals! This legislation gives authority to the Secretary of Homeland Security to expand required information on drivers' licenses, potentially including such biometric information as retina scans, finger prints, DNA information, and even Radio Frequency Identification (RFID) radio tracking technology. Including such technology as RFID means the federal government, as well as the governments of Canada and Mexico, could know where American citizens are at all times. . . . A national ID card will have the same effect as gun control laws: criminals will ignore it, while law abiding people will lose freedom. A national ID card offers us nothing more than a false sense of security, while moving us ever closer to a police state.

Note particularly that H.R. 418 provides that sensitive information on American citizens is to be shared with Canada and Mexico. Why would this legislation specify these two other nations? The ultimate goal of the power elite is a world Socialist government, which will be achieved by linking regional economic and then political arrangements. In the case of the United States, it was to be first linked economically with Canada and Mexico via NAFTA and then politically linked. In case you believe that political linkage is unimaginable, read Sean Gordon's "Group Looks at North America to Become One Country. Oh Really? What Have We Been Saying for Decades?" (*Toronto Star,* February 14, 2005) wherein he reveals the contents of a confidential internal summary from the first of three meetings of the Task Force on the Future of North America. He wrote that the task force "has considered a raft of bold proposals for an integrated North America, including a continental customs union, single passport and contiguous security perimeter." He then related that Council of Canadians chairperson Maude Barlow found the summary "disturbing" and "shocking," and he quoted her as saying, "What they envisage is a new North American reality with one passport, one immigration and refugee policy, one security regime, one foreign policy, one common set of environmental, health and safety standards."

The reason the Task Force is so important is that it is sponsored by the Council on Foreign Relations (CFR). And according to prominent CFR member Arthur Schlesinger, Jr., in *A Thousand Days* (and in *Tragedy and Hope* by Bill Clinton's mentor at Georgetown University, Prof. Carroll Quigley), the CFR is a "front" group for the power elite. The CFR was an outgrowth of Cecil Rhodes' plan "to take the government of the whole world." And from the "secret records" of Rhodes' plan that Prof. Quigley was able to obtain, one finds that on October 27, 1908, Lord Alfred Milner (who implemented Rhodes' plan) wrote to Arthur Glazebrook (leader of the Toronto Round Table Group until 1940), advising: "I think every member of your body should feel it his principal business to influence as many people as possible who are not of it and who do not know they are being influenced."

We as a people must resist (peacefully) the efforts of the power elite to diminish our God-given rights and liberties. As Daniel Webster reminded us in June 1834, "God grants liberty only to those who love it and are always ready to defend it." Unfortunately, the "liberty" which many Americans exercise today is the "liberty" of the French Revolution, which meant license to "do-your-own-thing" morally. And they are also increasingly accepting the "equality" of the French Revolution, which meant a leveling of the masses under the control of elite "philosopher kings," as Plato recommended in *The Republic*.

Though already quoted by many Christians in recent years, it is also appropriate to include here this biblical admonition in concluding part 9 of this series on mental health, education, and social control. As *The Holy Bible* states in 2 Chronicles 7:14, "If my people, which are called by my name, shall humble themselves, and pray, and seek my face, and turn from their wicked ways; then will I hear from heaven, and will forgive their sin, and will heal their land." Without turning from sin (e.g., fornication, selfishness, etc.) and repenting, God will not heal our land, and the power elite will continue to gain more and more control over our lives. We must therefore sincerely pray for restoration as truly one nation under God.

Part 10

In part 9 of this series, I mentioned that one means of bringing the public under control was to convince them that they are in need of the benevolent assistance of certain authority figures such as health professionals. You would think that under the guiding hand of these professionals, we would have the healthiest children ever. However, Ann Dachel, a member of the National Autism Association, said a speech therapist and nutritionist who works with children in hospitals and schools "brought up the fact that today's children are the sickest in history." Why in California has there been a six-fold increase in autism cases between 1987 and 2002? Could it be because of the vaccines these health professionals have promoted for children? Why do they give infants the Hepatitis B vaccine when it's "a disease transmitted through high-risk adult behavior involving intravenous drug use and unprotected sex," according to Evelyn Pringle in "Get Mercury Out of Vaccines—NOW" (*Independent Media TV*, March 16, 2005)? She interviewed Dr. Jay Gordon, a pediatrician who has been a consultant for CBS on children's programming, and he said the Hep B vaccine as well as the Meningitis vaccine may have autoimmune complications for children.

In part 9 of this series, I also mentioned that the mercury-based preservative thimerosal has been suspected as the source of some of the problems with vaccines. For several years, some drug companies have claimed they removed all mercury from their vaccines. But Health Advocacy in the

Public Interest (HAPI) recently sent four vaccines to be tested and found all four had some mercury, despite claims to the contrary by two of the vaccine manufacturers. According to Pringle's article, Boyd Haley (chemistry department chair at the University of Kentucky) told HAPI the claim of mercury-free vaccines "is false because mercury binds to the antigenic protein in the vaccine and cannot be completely filtered out 100%." In addition, Pringle writes that "drug companies admit that flu vaccines still contain an unsafe amount of thimerosal and the government still recommends flu vaccines for pregnant women and some children."

Another important aspect of social control I mentioned in part 9 of this series was H.R. 418 (The Real ID Act), which passed the U.S. House of Representatives on February 10, 2005, and would provide for a national ID via drivers' licenses and personal identification cards. It was hoped that the American public would be alarmed enough to prevent its passage by the U.S. Senate, but in a sneaky maneuver, H.R. 418 was incorporated in a rule for the Emerging Supplemental Wartime Appropriations Act (H.R. 1268) on March 16, 2005, which virtually guarantees its Senate passage due to all the "goodies" to be appropriated in the larger legislation. Welcome to the Brave New World !

Who has allowed the power elite to gain the social control over our lives they now enjoy? As a 1970 "Pogo" cartoon said, "We have met the enemy and he is us!" Many professing Christians and Jews for all practical purposes continue to allow abortion-on-demand, even though a simple congressional majority can limit federal courts' jurisdiction. Many professing Christians and Jews also believe that withholding food from Terri Schiavo is all right because that's just "allowing her to die" and not murdering her. But wouldn't it be considered murder to withhold food from people who are paralyzed or infants or anyone else who cannot feed themselves? While we teach children biblical morality at home, we continue to allow the public schools to indoctrinate our children with moral relativism. We allow chaplains in the military for the wiccan (witches) religion, while the Ten Commandments (but not pagan deities) are being removed from the public square. And we increasingly give huge amounts of money to the Chinese Communists by purchasing goods from China, even though we know they have slaughtered millions of innocent people, have forced women to have abortions, and have tortured Christians and other religious people. Would you fund the Nazis by buying their products? Then why do you buy products made in Communist China? Instead of saying "God bless America," we should be pleading for God to have mercy on America.

Just as the pagans of old worshipped the "sun god," today many Americans seem to worship the "fun god." They don't follow Philippians 4:8, which includes: ". . . whatsoever things are pure, whatsoever things are lovely, whatsoever things are of good report; if there be any virtue, and if there be any praise, think on these things." Instead, many Americans spend hour upon hour seeking to be entertained by lurid soap operas; mindless sitcoms; occultic books, cartoon shows and films; while tolerating immorality in movies, violent and crime-promoting videogames, depressing school literature requirements, sacrilegious art (some is government-funded), loud fractious music, and lewd dance. Unfortunately, many American Christians engage in or tolerate these activities because they believe they are "saved," having "accepted" Jesus as their Lord. Unfortunately, their pastors have not impressed upon them that this "acceptance" must be complete (*all* aspects of their lives). They ignore Matthew 25:44–46 where Jesus indicates that even those who call Him their "Lord" can "go away into everlasting punishment." And they also ignore William Penn's warning that "those who will not be governed by God will be ruled by tyrants."

Why do many Americans succumb to these temptations? One reason is that the government schools for decades have been indoctrinating students in the moral relativism of secular humanism under the facade of social and mental hygiene (for a good early history of the humanist mental hygiene movement, see *A Mind That Found Itself* by Clifford Beers, who in 1909 formed the U.S. National Committee for Mental Hygiene). In *Humanism: A New Religion* (1930), Charles Francis Potter proclaimed: "Education is thus a most powerful ally of humanism. What can the theistic Sunday schools, meeting for an hour once a week, and teaching only a fraction of the children, do to stem the tide of a five-day program of humanistic teaching?" Potter signed the first *Humanist Manifesto* (1933), which was co-authored by John Dewey (father of progressive education and honorary president of the National Education Association). The signers of the *Humanist Manifesto* said, "We consider the religious forms and ideas of our fathers no longer adequate," and they further stated, "We assume that humanism will take the path of social and mental hygiene." Their prognostication unfortunately was correct and their success regrettably great, especially via the government schools and as they undermined the family. On November 9, 1970, Ashley Montagu (1995 Humanist of the Year) told a thousand home economics teachers at Anaheim Convention Center: "The American family structure produces mentally ill children." Similarly, Montagu told seven thousand school board members in San Diego that "every child who enters school at the age of six in the United States is mentally ill because he comes to school with certain values he inherits from the family unit."

Undermining parental influence, schools began to instruct students in values based upon the principle that "It's your decision." In fact, that is the exact title of a chapter in the widely used textbook, *Contemporary Living*, which was first published in the 1980s. And beginning that decade, H. J. Blackham (a founder of the 4 million-member International Humanist and Ethical Union) wrote in *The Humanist* (September–October 1981) that if schools teach dependence (e.g., moral) on one's self, "they are more revolutionary than any conspiracy to overthrow the government." He was absolutely right, and we have been suffering the consequences ever since. Not long ago, the Josephson Institute of Ethics polled more than twenty thousand middle and high school students and found that an amazing 47 percent acknowledged that they had stolen something from a store in the past twelve months. Do public school teachers and secular humanists tell students to steal? No, but they do say the student is an autonomous moral decisionmaker who should make up her or his own mind about what is right or wrong based upon the situation. This could lead some students to say, "Most of the time I don't steal, but that store owner ripped me off on the price of a sweater, so in this situation I didn't see anything wrong with shoplifting something from him."

Another way to undermine the traditional American family has been to promote homosexuality. In September 1967, National Institute of Mental Health (NIMH) director Dr. Stanley Yolles appointed a pro-homosexual Task Force on Homosexuality. NIMH then funded the Kinsey Institute for Sex Research to conduct "the most comprehensive study ever done on homosexuals in the United States," and Tom Maurer (director of field research for the NIMH-funded project) said: "It is our hope that the study will produce data to change attitudes, laws, and ideas about homosexuals."

NIMH also funded (grant K6-MH-21, 775-01) B. F. Skinner (1972 Humanist of the Year) resulting in his *Beyond Freedom and Dignity* (1971) advocating man's freedom and dignity be replaced by collectivism. Congressman Cornelius Gallagher questioned the grant, and columnist Paul Scott in "Big Brother Develops Thought Control" (February 9, 1972), reported:

> To Representative Gallagher and a number of his colleagues in the House, all this adds up to the use of taxpayers' funds by the National Institutes of Health to promote Dr. Skinner's plan for having the government control our way of life. Gallagher also believes the grant indicates an emerging pattern of government-sponsored behavioral research the aim of which is to alter radically the values and the traditions of the nation, and with them our freedom. He contends that the logical conclusion of proposals like Skinner's must be a dictatorship under the control of those who believe in enforced population control and those who would pop pills into all of us to control our actions.

Returning to the subject of why many Americans succumb to the temptations listed earlier, Dr. Robert Assagioli, founder of psychosynthesis, believed it is possible to train the "will" (speaking on this at an Edgar Cayce conference was Dr. James Windsor, vice-president of the Mental Health Association of Virginia). Assagioli was a disciple of Alice Bailey (perhaps the leading occultist for the first half of the twentieth century), whose first works were published by Lucifer Publishing Company, and who emphasized the need for a "new world order" and "points of light" connected to "service."

A few years after Lucifer Publishing Company began publishing Bailey's works, Rockefeller Foundation president Max Mason on April 11, 1933, assured foundation trustees that in their program, "the Social Sciences will concern themselves with the rationalization of social control, . . . the control of human behavior." Then in the fall of 1937, the foundation gave a grant to Princeton University to study the influence of radio on different groups of listeners in the U.S. An Office of Radio Research was established with Paul Lazarsfeld (who would become president of the American Sociological Association) as director, and Frank Stanton (who would become president of CBS and on the editorial board of J. L. Moreno's journal, *Sociometry*) and Hadley Cantril (who would be chairman of the board of the Institute for International Social Research, 1955–1969) as associate directors. In 1935, Cantril had co-authored *Psychology of Radio* with Gordon Allport, who would be a leading agent in the U.S. for the Tavistock Institute, which in its *Human Relations* (Vol. II, No.3, 1949) published "Some Principles of Mass Persuasion." In the foreword of Cantril's *The Invasion from Mars: A Study in the Psychology of Panic* (Princeton University Press and Oxford University Press, 1940), one reads that the radio broadcast of "The War of the Worlds" provided "an unexpected 'experimental' situation. A special grant by the [Rockefeller] General Education Board made it possible to study the event which fitted so well into the whole frame of the Princeton Project."

Theodor Adorno was made chief of the music division of the Radio Project in February 1938, and in that year he wrote: ". . . It is contemporary [music] listening which has regressed, arrested at an infantile stage. . . . Their primitivism is not that of the undeveloped, but [rather] that of the forcibly retarded." Adorno believed that repetition (e.g., in music) could create popularity, and that one could change the culture away from "the authoritarian personality" (belief in traditional authority) toward the "revolutionary," liberating individuals from traditional values. He also believed that the mass media could be used for "opinion management," and that life will become "indistinguishable from the movies." Relevant to this last statement, CBS's "60 Minutes" on March 6, 2005, broadcast a segment regarding a teenager who had shot three police officers and had stolen a police car after repeatedly watching the videogame "Grand Theft Auto." The teen was quoted as saying "Life is like a videogame."

Some years after the Radio Project, Aldous Huxley authored *The Devils of Loudon* (1952) explaining how the masses could be conditioned, saying:

> Assemble a mob of men and women previously conditioned by a daily reading of newspapers; treat them to amplified band music, bright lights . . . and in next to no time you can reduce them to a state of almost mindless subhumanity. Never before have so few been in a position to make fools, maniacs, or criminals of so many.

Five years later, William Sargant wrote *Battle for the Mind* (British edition subtitle "The Mechanics of Indoctrination, Brainwashing and Thought Control"), in which he revealed that if certain "underlying physiological principles are once understood, it should be possible to get at the person, converting and maintaining him in his new belief by a whole variety of imposed stresses that end by altering his brain function." Sargant further claimed that the human brain

> is particularly sensitive to rhythmic stimulation by percussion and bright lights. . . . Belief can be implanted in people after brain function has been sufficiently disturbed by . . . induced fear, anger or excitement. Of the results caused by such disturbances, the most common one is temporarily impaired judgment and heightened suggestibility.

One means of implanting ideas in people who are subject to heightened suggestibility is via subliminal messages. Before you dismiss this as nonsensical, you need to consider a study by G. J. W. Smith, D. P. Spence, and G. S. Klein two years after Sargant's book was published. In "Subliminal Effects of Verbal Stimuli" (*Journal of Abnormal and Social Psychology*, 1959, pages 167–176), their study is described as follows:

A static, expressionless portrait of a man was flashed on a screen by Smith, Spence and Klein. They requested their subjects to note how the expression of the picture changed. They intermittently flashed the word "angry" on the screen, at exposures so brief that the subjects were consciously completely unaware of having seen the word. They tended, however, to see the face as becoming more angry. When the word "happy" was flashed on the screen in similar fashion, the viewers tended to see the face as becoming more happy. Thus they were clearly influenced by stimuli which registered at a subliminal level, stimuli of which the individual was not, and could not be, aware.

About twenty years later, the movie *Agency* in 1980 looked at the use of subliminal messages to influence public opinion regarding elections. In the movie, Mr. Quinn (played by Robert Mitchum) explains:

Let us enter the living room and we can enter the mind. It's power, our power. Public opinion is crucial. Someone must use a guiding hand. I've been hired, financed, . . . the names don't matter, though you might recognize some of them. Let's just call them an elite of power, or maybe an influential elite who understand the value of manipulating public opinion. . . . The public wants to be led. It needs to be led. We have long term plans.

Mitchum goes on to say how they will use this technique on children, too, because, "it's the next generation. They spend six hours a day watching television. We can plant seeds. . . . The concentration of power is healthy. It's like a vacuum cleaner that sucks up all the chaos and disorder and gets rid of it. It's as simple as getting a few messages across."

Before you dismiss the use of subliminal messages such as those in *Agency* to effect political campaigns, you need to remember that in the 2000 presidential campaign, the Republican National Committee ran a TV ad where in a fraction of a second, the word "RATS" was superimposed over the words, "The Gore Prescription Plan."

At about the same time as *Agency* was released, Flo Conway and Jim

Siegelman in their book, *Snapping: America's Epidemic of Sudden Personality Change* (1978), explained that "snapping" depicts

> the way in which intense experience may affect fundamental informa-
> tion-processing capacities of the brain. . . . The experience itself may . .
> . render the individual extremely vulnerable to suggestion. . . . TV stills
> the mind through repetition . . . in the . . . assault of momentary images
> upon vision. . . . Television also may be a potent neutralizing force of
> human thought and feeling. Its incessant transmissions of information
> physically trains an individual to hear and observe without stopping
> to think. . . . Our culture seems to be embarking on a destructive new
> course of manipulation and escapism, of human abdication.

To show how this repetitive assault of momentary images causing one not to think works, consider TV ads over the past twenty years. It used to be that such ads presented a message logically persuading consumers to purchase a particular product. However, over the past two decades, TV ads have increasingly used flashing lights and swirling images causing a subtle psychological effect researcher Bill Strittmatter has termed the "highlighted moment" principle. The principle works like a person's reaction to the sound of a gunshot. It's an unusual sound that most people do not commonly hear in their day-to-day experiences. When one hears or sees something unusual like this (e.g., a gunshot), something like a survival instinct begins to operate, and the hearer's or viewer's mind goes into an absorption-of- information mode rather than engaging in reflective analytical thought. Thus, if an ad on TV can fill thirty seconds with flashing and swirling images of a product, the viewer is almost constantly engaged in absorbing information about the product rather than thinking about the reasons he or she may or may not want to purchse it. Also, because the image is repeatedly flashed, it is registered in the brain more than once. The principle works like that described according to Sheila Ostrander and Lynn Schroeder with Nancy Ostrander in *Superlearning* (1979): "Yogis long ago developed special candles that give a faster flicker effect to change states of consciousness." The hyperactivity of the TV ads also has contributed to a feeling that the pace of life is faster now than several decades ago.

George Orwell in his book *1984* tried to warn us about this happening. When the heroic Winston in the book asserts that people will never succumb to Big Brother, he is informed by the antagonist O'Brien: "Suppose that we quicken the tempo of human life." The point Big Brother's agent O'Brien was making was that if the tempo of human life is speeded up, people have less time to reflect upon what is happening to them. They can then be more easily manipulated, and actually believe Big Brother's slogans such as "Ignorance is Strength" and "War is Peace."

Today, it looks like we are going to have a lot of "strength" (aka ignorance) given the way students have been dumbed down in the government schools. And it looks like we're going to have a lot of "peace" (aka war) given the Bush administration's varying rationales for going to war against Iraq. Was it because of weapons of mass destruction (WMD)? Or was it to overthrow a dictator? There are quite a few nations with WMD and dictators unfriendly toward the U.S., but we haven't invaded them. In *USA Today* (August 14, 2003) is a column by James Bovard titled "By accident or design, Bush hyped case for war," in which one reads: "Shortly after his inauguration, Bush joked to a crowd of Washington insiders: 'You can fool all of the people some of the time, and those are the ones you need to concentrate on.'" I would encourage Americans, though, not to be misled but to follow the advice of founding father John Adams written in the *Boston Gazette* in 1763: "Let us believe no man infallible or impeccable in government, any more than in religion; take no man's word against evidence, nor implicitly adopt the sentiments of others who may be deceived themselves, or may be interested in deceiving us."

With the quickened tempo of human life today, people unfortunately can be more easily misled and programmed for constant change. For example, on June 7, 1969, leading psychologist Carl Rogers delivered a graduation address at Sonoma State College, in which he proclaimed that "the man of the future . . . will be living his transient life mostly in temporary relationships. He must be able to establish closeness quickly. He must be able to leave the close relationships behind without excessive conflict or mourning." And in a 1976 textbook, *Core Concepts in Health,* by Paul Insel and Walton Roth, students are informed that "mental health belongs to people who can . . . be free and autonomous. . . . Healthy people know what their needs are and do whatever they must to satisfy them." Think of the profound implications and results of these statements by Rogers and the textbook authors (e.g., rise in divorce rate, sexual promiscuity, etc.). Nothing lasts (e.g., relationships, morality, truth, etc.)! This creates instability, so that people feel they can no longer cope, and therefore they become more willing to turn over authority to Big Brother and a one-world government. Psychiatrist and first director-general of the World Health Organization Brock Chisholm (1959 Humanist of the Year) said, "Universal mental health means one world." And to the power elite, only those who accept a one-world government will be considered to have proper mental health.

Part 11

As indicated before, the one-world government will be Socialist, having been brought about by a Hegelian synthesis of western Capitalism and eastern Communism, linking regional economic arrangements such as NAFTA, the European Union, and others. As Prof. Robert A. Pastor wrote in the January–February 2004 edition of the Council on Foreign Relations' *Foreign Affairs,* "NAFTA was merely the first draft of an economic constitution for North America." The one-world government will also be feudalistic in nature, as Arthur S. Miller in *Democratic Dictatorship: The Emergent Constitution of Control* (1981) described a "new feudal order" controlled by elitists. Miller also assessed that

> dictatorship will come—is coming—but with the acquiescence of the people, who subconsciously probably want it. The Grand Inquisitor likely was correct: People want material plenty and mysticism, not perfect freedom. Freedom is an intolerable burden. . . . The ideologist for the development is B. F. Skinner. The goal is "predictable" man—a person who conceives of freedom in Hegelian terms. Americans are moving into a Skinnerian world, one in which they "will no longer know, or care, whether they are volunteers or conscripts. The distinctions will have vanished" (Peter Schrag, *Mind Control,* 1978).

Miller followed this work with *Secret Constitution and the Need for Consti-*

tutional Change (1987), expressing thanks to the Rockefeller Foundation for its help. In this book, Miller declared that

> a pervasive system of thought control exists in the United States. . . . The citizenry is indoctrinated by employment of the mass media and the system of public education, . . . people are told what to think about. . . . The old order is crumbling. . . . Nationalism should be seen as a dangerous social disease. . . . A new vision is required to plan and manage the future, a global vision that will transcend national boundaries and eliminate the poison of nationalistic "solutions." . . . A new constitution is necessary. . . . Americans really have no choice, for constitutional alteration will come whether or not it is liked or planned for. . . . Ours is the age of the planned society. . . . No other way is possible.

We are supposed to be a government of, by, and for the people. However, we are not actually in control of our lives, but rather a power elite constitutes an invisible government which really controls us and will plan the direction of our society. If you doubt this, on April 19, 1906, President Theodore Roosevelt revealed: "Behind the ostensible government sits enthroned an invisible government owing no allegiance and acknowledging no responsibility to the people."

Because we are to be a "planned society," a major part of the power elite's plan involves what to do about the sharp increase in the proportion of elderly in the U.S. This is one possible reason "death education" has been promoted over the past few decades in our schools. In 1975 author Erica Carle wrote of her concern that

> the influence of the Education Commission of the States will force the teaching of *death education* in our schools. *Death education* (Thanatology) was one of the main subjects covered at a convention of the newly-formed Wisconsin Secondary School Psychology Teachers which was held on October 30, 1975. . . . The Euthanasia Education Council, . . . Planned Parenthood, and many, many more are cooperating. Your sons and daughters do not have to be happy, carefree, well balanced and

mentally sound any longer. Their minds can be controlled, corrupted and emotionalized by being forced to dwell on suicide, euthanasia, abortion, mercy killing, cancer, leukemia, murder, grief, bereavement, old age, fear, funerals, and capital punishment. The attitudes of students on any related subject can be thoroughly probed and recorded in the computer records. . . . The following are questions from the questionnaire we received at the convention: . . . To what extent do you believe in life after death? To what extent do you believe in reincarnation? How often do you think about your own death? If you could choose, when would you die? (Note: Will this choice be recorded and used as permission to cause death at a later date?) For whom or what might you be willing to kill another person? How often have you seriously contemplated committing suicide?

About a week later, the *Milwaukee County News* (November 6, 1975) reported that one student slipped into a coma and died after death education in her junior high class. Doctors were unable to help her condition! They were baffled by her complete lack of will to live or even to attempt to live.

One reason for all of this focus being placed upon death has been to condition the populace to accept euthanasia. In Robert Hugh Benson's *Lord of the World*, which was written in 1907, he said that by the late 1990s there would be ministers of euthanasia (like Dr. Jack Kevorkian). Benson also said the Communist movement would come to the fore in 1917 (the exact year of the Russian Revolution), and that the final scheme of western free trade would occur in 1989.

Benson's father, Edward White Benson, founded the Cambridge Ghost Society in 1851 (with members such as B. F. Westcott and Fenton John Antony Hort) before becoming the Archbishop of Canterbury. The Ghost Society was the forerunner of the Society for Psychical Research (SPR), co-founded in 1882 by Henry Sidgwick, who tutored Bertrand Russell and whose sister Mary married Edward White Benson. And Henry Sidgwick married Eleanor Balfour, sister of Arthur Balfour who became president of the SPR, as did William James, the father of American psychology (Sigmund Freud and Carl Jung would become corresponding members of the SPR—see letter below from Jung to H. G. Wells about the latter's book *The Open Conspiracy*). Arthur Balfour's brother Gerald (also a president of the SPR) was Emily Lytton Lutyens' brother-in-law, and she was the granddaughter of occultist and alchemist Lord Edward Bulwer-Lytton and a disciple of theosophist Annie Besant (who wore a swastika pendant and co-edited *Lucifer* magazine with Madame Helena Petrovna Blavatsky, the founder of the Theosophical Society). Lutyens was also foster-mother of Jiddu Krishnamurti, who was promoted by Annie Besant as Lord Maitreya (supposedly "the Christ" of the New Age).

According to Bill Clinton's mentor at Georgetown University, Prof.

Dr. med. C. G. Jung LL. D.

888 ...
Küsnacht-Zürich

June 11th 1928

My dear Mr. Wells:

I thank You for sending me your very interesting and suggestive book "The open Conspiracy", and I marvel that your interest is still going out to this fiction of a world that apparently wants to be improved. They are at this job since two thousand years and it is still doubtful wether they have succeeded or not. Well, let us try anyhow!

I am going to send you my new English publication as soon as it is out.

Very sincerely yours

C. G. Jung.

Carroll Quigley in *The Anglo-American Establishment*, the SPR was "one of the enduring creations of the Cecil Bloc," which was headed by British prime minister Sir Robert Gascoyne-Cecil (Lord Salisbury) and which included many of the power elite from which Cecil Rhodes formed his secret "Society of the Elect" to "take the government of the whole world," in Rhodes' own words. Rhodes' mentor, John Ruskin, was a member of the SPR and has a swastika on his gravestone. Members of the American SPR included author Mark Twain, attorney Clarence Darrow, the "father of progressive education" John Dewey, and environmentalist Gifford Pinchot (Skull & Bones member) who was a vice-president of the First International Congress of Eugenics in 1912 along with Winston Churchill, Alexander Graham Bell, and Harvard University president (1869–1909) Charles Eliot. Former British prime minister William Gladstone was a member of the SPR, and Arthur Balfour in 1902 became British prime minister after Lord Salisbury, who was the brother of Arthur and Gerald Balfour's mother. Could it be that Robert Hugh Benson's amazingly accurate forecasts in *Lord of the World* in 1907 were actually a result of his hearing the plans of these powerful people when he was a boy?

How will the planned global society come about in the future? It might happen something like this. In the past, U.S. policy has been to support Third World dictators with whom we made deals. If there was a democratically elected government that did not obey the will of certain American transnational corporations, it was toppled (e.g., Iran in the early 1950s when they nationalized their oil and the CIA had them overthrown). Now, however, the policy is to put in place democratically elected rulers beholden to the U.S. (e.g., Hamid Karzai in Afghanistan) and who will make deals (Karzai was a UNOCAL consultant and pipeline deals have been made). A number of American transnational corporations (e.g., Bechtel, Halliburton, etc.) are happy with this arrangement, but there is a realization that democratically elected governments eventually tend to become nationalistic. The power elite intends to control that by economically entangling the foreign governments in the World Trade Organization and by getting them in debt, so that it will be economic suicide for them not to submit "voluntarily" to the power elite's will.

The people of America and the world will be told that what is occurring is a positive movement toward global integration. Regarding the Clinton Global Initiative conference in New York City on September 22–24, 2005, former President Clinton wrote a letter concerning "the challenges of global interdependence" and said: "I am excited about this opportunity to work with you in an effort to move the world from an unstable interdependence toward an integrated global economy of shared responsibilities, shared opportunities and shared values in the years to come." The power elite will use networks of like-minded globalists to further its aims. These include Bill Clinton and his network of Rhodes Scholars, as well as the Bush family and its Skull & Bones network along with members of other Yale University secret societies. Do you really think President Bush's recent appointments of Yale's Psi Upsilon (founded as a secret society in the 1830s) members John Negroponte to head the Department of Homeland Security and Porter Goss to head the CIA were coincidences? Another Psi Upsilon member (and in the same year's membership photo as Negroponte and Goss) is President Bush's uncle William H. T. Bush, who has made a lot of money from the Iraq war.

The press/media will also be used by the power elite in selecting what information the public receives and doesn't receive. Remember that in the late 1940s, the CIA under Operation Mockingbird began infiltrating the press.

Food will even be a weapon used by the power elite to control the population of the world. In fact, it has already been used as a weapon. On December 10, 1974, the National Security Council's NSSM 200, "Implications of Worldwide Population Growth for U.S. Security and Overseas Interests," is marked "classified" and "confidential." It was proposed by Secretary of State Henry Kissinger and was given final approval by National Security Adviser Brent Scowcroft. The document stated that

> if future numbers are to be kept within reasonable bounds, it is urgent that measures to reduce fertility be started and made effective in the 1970s and 1980s. . . . [Financial] assistance will be given to other countries, considering such factors as population growth. . . . Food and

agricultural assistance is vital for any population sensitive development strategy. . . . Allocation of scarce resources should take account of what steps a country is taking in population control. . . . There is an alternative view that mandatory programs may be needed. . . .

Although the power elite will resort to mandatory measures if necessary, they prefer creating situations in which the public believes it is voluntarily accepting something. For example, concerning mental health screening, insurance companies may say your insurance premiums will increase if you are not screened. Therefore, people "voluntarily" will submit to mental health screenings to prevent an increase in payments. In addition, there are current discussions about future means-testing for Social Security, and whether one has had a mental health screening could also be added as a criteria for level of Social Security payments to individuals.

The only thing that might threaten the power elite's plan will be religious (e.g., Christian, Islamic, Jewish, etc.) fundamentalists, who are already being branded as "extremists" who are "intolerant" of others. This is designed to discredit and marginalize them. And if necessary, they will be branded as "mentally ill." In *The Case Against Religion: A Psychotherapist's View* (1968), sexologist Albert Ellis (1971 Humanist of the Year) proclaimed that

Religion is . . . directly opposed to the goals of mental health. . . . It encourages a fanatic, obsessive-compulsive kind of commitment that is, in its own right, a form of mental illness. . . . This close connection between mental illness and religion is inevitable and invariant. . . . In the final analysis, then, religion is neurosis.

There has been support in the media for this attitude as well. Recently, Bill Maher, host of HBO's "Real Time With Bill Maher," said on MSNBC's "Scarborough Country" that "Religion stops people from thinking. I think it justifies crazies. . . . I think religion is a neurological disorder." You may say this was just the ranting of one man, but the point is that he wasn't fired for saying this! Don Wildmon, chairman of the American Family

Association, explained: "Had Maher said such things about homosexuals, he would have been immediately fired. But because he was speaking of Christians, his bigotry was acceptable to HBO, owned by Time-Warner, Inc." (*www.afa.net/hbobillmaher.asp*).

Social control also will be exercised via education. In the late 1960s, the Wisconsin Social Studies Curriculum Committee produced *Knowledge Processes and Values in the New Social Studies* (Bulletin No. 185, 1968–70), in which one could read:

> A child generally comes to school with what R. J. Havighurst calls an authoritarian conscience acquired from his parents through a progression of punishments and rewards. He soon learns that he is not equipped to deal with all the new situations which confront him. Peers and teachers join and sometimes supplant parents in helping him to find solutions which are often in conflict with those offered by his parents. His task, then, is to change from this early authoritarian conscience to a rational one.

A couple of years later, Solveig Eggerz wrote "Psychiatry in the Classroom," which was published in the May 1972 edition of *Private Practice, The Journal of Socio-Economic Medicine* (published by the Congress of County Medical Societies). In this article, she related that Health, Education and Welfare secretary Elliot Richardson told a National Education Association (NEA) convention: "It may very well be that the teachers are potentially our largest cadre of mental health personnel." She then informed the reader that Robert F. Peck and James V. Mitchell stated in an NEA booklet that "the school has a major stake in repairing damaged mental health and in enhancing good mental health." And she explained that Peck and Mitchell advocated that the teacher practice extensive mental health measurement in the classroom.

This all fit neatly with the NEA's forecast, as its publication *Today's Education* in its January 1969 edition published Harold and June Shane's "Forecast for the '70s," a digest of many articles, in which one finds the following comments:

Ten years hence it should be more accurate to term him [the teacher] a "learning clinician." This title is intended to convey the idea that schools are becoming "clinics" whose purpose is to provide individualized psychosocial "treatment" for the student, thus increasing his value both to himself and to society. . . . [Children would] become the objects of [biochemical] experimentation.

In the late 1960s, the NEA also had promoted "sensitivity training," which was characterized in its 1962 publication *Issues in (Human Relations) Training* as fitting into "a context of institutional influence procedures which includes coercive persuasion in the form of thought reform or brainwashing." According to Solveig Eggerz in her article mentioned above, Paul Hummel, an associate professor at the University of Hawaii, said that the deeper forms of sensitivity training

can have such traumatic effects as to cause complete mental breakdown in individuals. In many cases the loyalties of persons have changed completely. School children lose all respect for their parents, church and country. They gain a group dependency and are willing to follow the group direction whether it involves rioting, the use of drugs or any other type of extreme behavior.

Does this sound like what has been happening in American society over the past several decades?

The NEA publication *Issues In (Human Relations) Training* mentioned above also includes information about "change-agent skills" and "unfreezing, changing and refreezing" attitudes. As I related in part 4 (found in the companion book) on mental health, education and social control, NEA president Catherine Barrett in the February 10, 1973, edition of *Saturday Review of Education* declared:

Dramatic changes in the way we raise our children in the year 2000 are indicated, particularly in terms of schooling. . . . We will need to recognize that the so-called "basic skills," which currently represent nearly the total effort in elementary schools, will be taught in one-quarter of the present school day. . . . When this happens—and it's near—the teacher can rise to his true calling. More than a dispenser of information, the teacher will be a conveyor of values, a philosopher. . . . We will be agents of change.

Thus, NEA "change agents" were determined to be conveyors of a new set of values to students. And how would they accomplish their goals? After students' values were unfrozen via a values clarification process destroying the concept of moral absolutes, the students' values were then changed via sensitivity training to accept "common values" (those values we all have in common), which were then refrozen via reinforcement mechanisms like Pavlov's dogs.

In the future, those disagreeing with the need for "common values" will be labeled as in need of mental health services, because they will be identified as having "oppositional deficit disorder." According to the *Diagnostic and Statistical Manual of Mental Disorders* (found in social service agencies, schools, etc.) code 313.81 DSM IV, "oppositional deficit disorder" includes arguing with adults (e.g., teachers), acting angry, refusing to obey (e.g., teachers), annoying other people, or blaming others for misbehavior. Thus, you can see how easy it is to identify someone as having a mental disorder and in need of mental health services.

And the changing of values is not just limited to students, as the NTL Institute of Applied Behavioral Science (which was the NEA division that produced *Issues in [Human Relations] Training*) on September 19–22, 2004, co-sponsored the Second International Conference on Appreciative Inquiry (for "bold innovators who want to harness the power of positive change in their organizations"), including a roundtable session on "Creating a Collaborative Community-Based Solution for Mental Health." NTL describes itself as "the premier source for transformational change," and their program registration form requests participants to sign a statement that "I understand that my participation in this NTL program may involve considerable stress." In fact, they have stated: "Persons who are experiencing personal, emotional crises should forego attendance at NTL programs."

President Bush's New Freedom Commission on Mental Health (NFC-MH) had appointed subcommittees, one of which on February 5, 2003, issued a report titled "Promoting, Preserving and Restoring Children's Mental Health." Concerning the broadening of the definition of "mental health," the report stated: "Federal and state governments should promote a broader concept of 'mental health' services for children and adolescents with emotional disorders and their families." To give a sense of urgency, the report said:

> Mental health problems among children and adolescents constitute a public health crisis for our nation. . . . The extent, severity, and far-reaching consequences of mental health problems in children and adolescents make it imperative that our nation adopt a comprehensive, systematic, public health approach to improving the mental health status of children.

The subcommittee report recommended screening of children from birth to five years old for social and emotional development. And to be sure lots of taxpayers' dollars are available, it recommended a plan for Medicaid to pay for services. This is especially important for the drug companies, as antidepressant and antipsychotic drugs can be very expensive. In a press release on July 22, 2003, the NFCMH recommended redesigning mental health systems in all states, and said: "Achieving this goal will require . . . a greater focus on mental health care in institutions such as schools, child welfare programs, and the criminal and juvenile justice systems. The goal is integrated care that can screen, identify, and respond to problems early."

The rate of increase in prescribed drugs for children has also been alarming. According to Erica Goode's "Sharp Rise Found in Psychiatric Drugs for the Very Young" (*New York Times,* February 23, 2000), a recent study found that

> the use of stimulants—most commonly methylphenidate, the generic form of Ritalin—increased twofold to threefold for children ages 2

through 4 from 1991 to 1995. . . . Dr. Joseph Coyle, chairman of psychiatry at Harvard Medical School, commented that the normal behavior of many 2-year-olds and 3-year-olds looks a lot like attention deficit hyperactivity disorder. "These interventions are occurring at a critical time in brain development," said Dr. Coyle, "and we don't know what the consequences are."

The number of children on antidepressants increased by over 500 percent from 1999 to 2003. There were over 7 million prescriptions written for Eli Lilly's Zyprexa in 2002, and *The New York Times* reported that 70 percent of Zyprexa purchased in the U.S. in 2003 were paid for by Medicaid and other federal programs. You may recall that after George H. W. Bush left the CIA in 1977, he joined Eli Lilly's board of directors.

For *Online Journal,* Evelyn Pringle wrote "Drug makers to profit from Bush scheme to label kids mentally ill" (March 15, 2005), for which she interviewed Dr. Jane Orient, executive director of the Association of American Physicians and Surgeons (AAPS), about "this latest profiteering scheme." Dr. Orient commented: "Teams of experts are awaiting an infusion of cash. They'll be ensconced in your child's school before you even know it. A bonus is that your little darlings will probably give them quite a lot of information about you also, and then you can receive therapy you didn't know you needed." Dr. Orient further explained that children will be asked if their parents "ever spank them? Have politically incorrect attitudes? Use forbidden words? Own a gun? Smoke cigarettes, especially indoors? Read extremist literature? Refuse to recycle? Prepare for a knock at the door."

Pringle added that

According to the University of Wisconsin-Whitewater Student Health Center, privacy rights are essentially being ignored. The center is telling patients that if government agencies want to see their medical records, they get to review them without a patient's knowledge or consent. "By law we cannot reveal when we have disclosed such information to the government," the center advised.

In a more recent article, "Bush Puppets Push for New Law to Protect Drug Companies" (*Independent Media TV,* April 18, 2005), Pringle described the dangers associated with the antidepressants so many students are taking. She noted that one of the Columbine killers, Eric Harris, had been taking Luvox, which lists adverse reactions as: "FREQUENT: amnesia, apathy, hyperkinesis, hypokinesis, manic reaction, myoclonus, psychotic reaction." She also noted that Jeff Weise, who recently killed nine persons and himself in Red Lake, Minnesota, was taking Prozac. Moreover, Pringle wrote that

> in addition to SSRI (selective serotonin reuptake inhibitors) antidepressants being dangerous, these expensive drugs are a rip-off because studies have shown they do not even work on children. The August 10, 2004, *Washington Post* reported, "Two-thirds of the trials conducted by drug manufacturers found that the medications performed no better than sugar pills, but details of the negative trials were kept from doctors and parents."

The alternative to drugs, psychotherapy, is no better either. The best-known early research on this was by Hans J. Eysenck, who in "Psychotherapy, Behavior Therapy, and the Outcome Problem," British Medical Association (BMA) Audio Cassette/T-308 (New York: Guilford Publications, 1979), found that after examining eight thousand cases, "roughly two-thirds of a group of neurotic patients will recover or improve to a marked extent within about two years of the onset of their illness, whether they are treated by means of psychotherapy or not." Moreover, in *Psychotherapy Research: Methodological and Efficacy Issues* (1982) by the American Psychiatric Association Commission on Psychotherapies, one reads that "unequivocal conclusions about causal connections between treatment and outcome may never be possible in psychotherapy research."

Part 12

At the end of part 11 of this series, I referred to SSRIs (selective serotonin reuptake inhibitors) as being dangerous. According to Dr. Ann Blake Tracy, director of the International Coalition for Drug Awareness, SSRIs increase serotonin while decreasing the metabolism of serotonin. Horror stories of homicide and suicide abound concerning children and adults on SSRI antidepressants, with people on the drugs saying what they were doing didn't seem real. In Evelyn Pringle's article, "Bush-backed drug marketing schemes" (*Online Journal,* April 25, 2005), Dr. Tracy explained that SSRIs suppress

> the REM state or dream state [of sleep]. . . . These drugs allow a person to be awake but at any time they can slip into the REM state. This is why people often discuss how they couldn't tell the difference between the dream and reality. These drugs are horribly damaging to the entire system.

Dr. Tracy also forecast that if President Bush's New Freedom Commission on Mental Health recommendations result in more children being given these dangerous SSRIs, then we had better prepare for even more horror stories of death in the future. SSRIs are banned for children in the United Kingdom, and in February 2005, Adderall was taken off the market in

Canada because it was linked to twenty sudden deaths (fourteen were children) and a dozen strokes.

According to Encarnacion Pyle's article, "Even babies getting treated as mentally ill" (*Columbus Dispatch,* April 25, 2005),

> Doctors prescribed sedatives and powerful, mood-altering medications for nearly 700 babies and toddlers on Medicaid last summer. . . . "It's shocking," said Dr. Ellen Bassuk, associate professor of psychiatry at Harvard Medical School. "Who's really being helped by these children being drugged? The babies? Or their caregivers? These medications are not benign; they can give dangerous side effects, and have to be closely monitored."

Pyle's article went on to describe how Ohio parents Mike and Janet Hall's daughter Stephanie had been placed on Ritalin after her first grade teacher pressured them into drugging her. Stephanie died of a heart attack in January 1996, the morning after a doctor doubled her daily dose.

Americans should protest the widespread drugging of our children, and resist any efforts by the power elite to control us by increasing the number of our youth placed on dangerous SSRIs. Of course, the power elite understands there will always be a rebellious remnant opposing their will. However, tactics have already been developed for handling protesters, and the complacent American public (and that includes some of you who are reading this) has apparently decided it's not worth the effort to do anything about these infringements upon our rights. After all, haven't most Americans been complacent about Congress "robbing" from their Social Security so-called "trust fund" for years? Had the American people held Congress accountable for this "robbery," there probably wouldn't be a crisis in Social Security funds for the future.

How did this happen? Basically, the power elite "turned off" the average American regarding protests, causing them to see protesters as radical extremists with whom they would not want to be associated. In this regard, the power elite actually supported radical protesters. And if you doubt this, then read James Simon Kunen's *The Strawberry Statement* (1968), in which the author tells of an SDS (Students for a Democratic Society) strategy meeting he attended where a student was giving a report about an SDS convention the student had recently attended, and the student's report revealed that

> men from Business International Roundtables . . . tried to buy up a few radicals. Those men are the world's industrialists and they convene to decide how our lives are going to go. They're the left wing of the ruling class. They offered to finance our demonstrations in Chicago. We were also offered ESSO [Rockefeller] money. They want us to make a lot of radical commotion so they can look more in the center as they move more to the left.

More recently concerning how the power elite handles protest movements, Lewis Lapham related in "Crowd Control" (*Harper's Magazine,* October 2004) that around May 2002,

> the Department of Homeland Security issued an all-points bulletin advising the nation's law enforcement agencies to keep a sharp watch for any citizens who might have "expressed dislike of attitudes and decisions of the U.S. government." . . . On the [April 15, 2000] night preceding the Washington protest against the policies of the World Bank/IMF, city police raided an assembly point on Florida Avenue. Supposedly responding to a complaint about zoning and fire-code violations, they confiscated the next day's handbills and parade puppets. . . . In Washington on September 27, 2002, the police arrested 400 people in Pershing Park for "failure to obey" an unspecified order that was never given. Restrained in "flexicuffs" that tethered one wrist to the opposite ankle, the detainees could neither stand up nor lie down. . . . In October 2003 the FBI sent a memorandum to 15,000 local law enforcement agencies citing as examples of potential criminal activities the use of tape recorders and video cameras as well as wearing sunglasses or headscarves. . . . In some jurisdictions cell phones qualify as "instru-

ments of crime" and, if it so pleases the arresting officer, the possession of one constitutes a misdemeanor.

An additional tactic of the power elite to thwart the efforts of those opposing their will is the formation of "controlled opposition" groups. These are used to draw out, monitor, control, and if necessary discredit any opponents. There are basically two ways of doing this, with chemicals and psychologically. Under the CIA's infamous MK-Ultra program in the 1950s, there was a May 5, 1955, document indicating its Technical Services Staff/Chemical Division is partly "devoted to the discovery of the following materials and methods: Substances which will promote illogical thinking and impulsiveness to the point where the recipient would be discredited in public. . . ."

Psychologically, the means can be rather basic. First, an individual may be taunted until he or she reacts with an emotional outburst, and then he or she is accused of "acting like a maniac" (a mental health problem). Another means involves a political candidate, for example, having an opponent who is so extreme that the public feels it has no choice but to vote for the original candidate. An example of this might be if a presidential candidate wins election even though, as governor of a state, he executed a born-again Christian woman who was a model prisoner bringing other prisoners to Christ according to her warden, while at the same time as governor the candidate commuted to a life sentence another prisoner who murdered many people, including a little boy (the son of the host of TV's "America's Most Wanted") after that prisoner and his homosexual "companion" abused the little boy. Then as president, he appoints homosexuals to prominent positions; his federal agents raid a church in Indiana arresting the pastor and seizing the property (even though the previous very liberal president did not take such action against the pastor and church); a terrorist attack that he could have easily prevented occurs killing thousands of Americans; he refers positively to Ozzy Osbourne's music (e.g., "Sabbath Bloody Sabbath" and "Facing Hell") which is occultic, demonic, and praises Lucifer/Satan; he dramatically increases federal domestic funding of Planned Parenthood over the previous liberal president's funding; he supports a pro-abortion rights and pro-homosexual rights Republican candidate for the U.S. Senate from Pennsylvania while opposing a strong pro-life Republican candidate; and he flashes his middle finger at a TV camera in late October 2004 before making an announcement regarding a sports event. How could such a candidate garner the votes of enough Christians to win re-election? Perhaps he would squeak out a victory by just one state (Ohio) only if his opponent is the most liberal member of the U.S. Senate (pro-abortion rights and pro-homosexual rights), from Massachusetts, and a friendly member of the same secret society (Skull & Bones) as the president, and if his opponent conveniently runs a lackluster campaign.

If any future terrorist acts occur, they will be used by the power elite to cause the public "voluntarily" to request greater control over us by the power elite for the security of all in the form of a one-world government. By the way, haven't you wondered why there hasn't been a terrorist attack in the U.S. in the years since the 9/11 attacks in 2001? If tons of drugs are still bypassing our security checkpoints into this country, isn't it logical that at least small amounts of biological or chemical weapons could be slipped in as well? Think about why this hasn't happened if it would be relatively easy for terrorists to have done it! And while you're at it, also think about the following statement by longtime Middle East CIA agent Robert Baer in his *See No Evil* (2002): "The other day a reporter friend told me that one of the highest-ranking CIA officials had said to him, off the record, that when the dust finally clears, Americans will see that September 11 was a triumph for the intelligence community not a failure."

Prior to the terrorist attacks of September 11, 2001, there was a bill introduced in Congress that sought to do what the "REAL ID Act" (mentioned in part 10 of this series) seeks to do, transforming states' drivers' licenses into *de facto* national ID cards. At the time, an outraged public forced Congress to back down and the bill died. However, after the attacks of 9/11, the U.S. House of Representatives passed H.R. 418 ("The REAL ID Act") as did the U.S. Senate on May 10, 2005, and U.S. Rep. Ron Paul warned of the consequences in his weekly column for May 9, 2005, titled "National ID Cards Won't Stop Terrorism or Illegal Immigration."

He projected that

> within two years every American will need a conforming national ID
> card to participate in ordinary activities. This REAL ID Act establishes
> a massive, centrally-coordinated database of highly personal information
> about American citizens. . . . The legislation also grants open-ended
> authority to the Secretary of Homeland Security to require biometric
> information on IDs in the future. This means your harmless looking
> driver's license could contain a retina scan, fingerprints, DNA informa-
> tion, or radio frequency technology. . . . A careful reading also reveals
> that states will be required to participate in the "Drivers License Agree-
> ment," which . . . creates a massive database of sensitive information
> on American citizens that can be shared with Canada and Mexico! . .
> . Nationalizing standards for drivers' licenses and birth certificates in a
> federal bill creates a national ID system, pure and simple. . . . Any refusal
> [by states] to comply would mean their residents could not get a job,
> receive Social Security, or travel by plane. . . . One overriding point has
> been forgotten: Criminals don't obey laws! . . . National ID cards will
> be used to track the law-abiding masses, not criminals.

Of course, for Big Brother to track everyone, it will be necessary to have
the ability to locate individuals at any given moment. In that regard, it
should soon be possible to link GPS (global positioning satellite) technology with RFID (radio frequency identification) technology. For example,
some Japanese schoolchildren are now wearing tennis shoes (made in the
U.S.) that can be tracked by GPS. The implanted device is still too large
to be put in most personal apparel, though, but Checkpoint Systems, Inc.,
has developed "Liberty" portals which can tell if something on your person
with an RFID chip has passed through a doorway of a store. Therefore,
with GPS and RFID technology, Big Brother will soon be able to tell
exactly where you are at any given time.

And if anyone needs "assistance" in accepting a one-world government,
the means of accomplishing that have been available to Big Brother for
quite some time. Concerning the power elite's ability to control someone's

memory, in *Prisoner No.7: Rudolf Hess* by Lt. Col. Eugene K. Bird, one reads in the chapter titled "A Secret Drug" that Dr. John Rawlings Rees (mentioned earlier in this series of articles on mental health, education and social control) of Tavistock and the British War Ministry examined Nazi prisoner Rudolf Hess thirty-five times. Rees and his associates via chemicals caused Hess' memory to fail and then "explained that they could bring back the memory with an injection" of the narcotic Evipan. Hess was told "that while under its influence, he would remember the past he had forgotten." Hess was injected on May 7, 1944.

Concerning the power elite's ability to control someone's behavior, I have already explained in part 6 of this series how the Nazis used sodium fluoride in water supplies to cause those in their occupied territories to become less resistant to domination. And I further explained how in the late 1940s, President Harry Truman appointed Oscar Ewing to head the Federal Security Agency which included the Public Health Service, and Ewing hired Edward Bernays for a propaganda campaign to place fluoride in Americans' supply of drinking water (note on the label of a can of sodium fluoride from the 1950s reproduced below. It states, "WARNING: May Be Fatal If Swallowed").

More recently concerning the power elite's ability to control behavior, IBM's 2020 neural chip implant has already been tested on unsuspecting

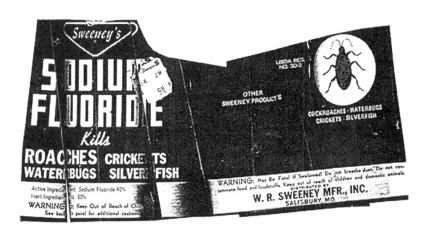

(sedated before implanting) Soledad prisoners, and it provides a visual and audio record of all events in which the subjects are involved. It has been used to reduce aggression, to make the subjects lethargic, or to disable them. Similarly, in the mid-1980s, Dr. Sigmund Gieriech of Britain's Whitehall Scientific Institute for the Betterment of Humanity developed a tiny computer (Electro Computer Brain Enhancer—ECBE) which fits at the base of one's brain, attaching to its electrical system and monitoring brain waves. Experiments on prisoners at Birmingham, England's maximum security Rehabilitation Center for the criminally insane were successful (whenever a criminal thought occurred, a jolt of electricity reminded the prisoner not to do what he was thinking about). Civilian volunteer Dr. Ormond Shell also carried one in his brain and related, "I don't even know that it's in my head. It stores a list of mathematical formulas for me. . . . It certainly has made my work easier. I think soon there will be models out that anyone can use. It really is something that everyone should have." Perhaps Big Brother will see to it that everyone does indeed have an ECBE, so that if you fail to accept the one-world government, all Big Brother has to do is give you an electrical jolt via the ECBE and you will no longer have such "negative" thoughts! And to track each person's sensation from an ECBE or anything else, by A.D. 2025 British Telecom's artificial-life team headed by Dr. Chris Winter expects to have developed a small computer chip (implanted behind the eye) that will record a person's every sensation, which can then be played back by a computer.

If you think the possibility of the power elite using ECBEs to give electrical jolts to those objecting to their will is far-fetched, you need to realize that for many years leading Socialists have advocated killing people to fulfill their plans. In *The Intelligent Woman's Guide to Socialism and Capitalism* (1928), Fabian Socialist author George Bernard Shaw explained that "under Socialism you would not be allowed to be poor. You would be forcibly fed, clothed, lodged, taught, and employed whether you liked it or not. If it were discovered that you had not the character and industry enough to be worth all this trouble, you might possibly be executed in a kindly manner." About twenty-five years later, Fabian Socialist Bertrand Russell in *The Impact of Science on Society* postulated that

Population can be kept from increasing. . . . Perhaps bacteriological war may prove effective. If a Black Death could be spread throughout the world once in every generation, survivors could procreate freely without making the world too full. . . . A scientific world society cannot be stable unless there is a world government. . . . This authority should deal out the world's food to the various nations in proportion to their population at the time of the establishment of the authority. If any nation subsequently increased its population, it should not on that account receive any more food.

The advocacy of killing people has not been limited to Fabian Socialists, as in the November 1991 edition of the *UNESCO Courier,* Jacques Cousteau was quoted as declaring: "It's terrible to have to say this. World population must be stabilized and to do that, we must eliminate 350,000 people per day. This is so horrible to contemplate that we shouldn't even say it. But the general situation in which we are involved is lamentable." And six years later, the Minneapolis *Star-Tribune* on January 12, 1997, published "The Methusaleh dilemma: Can America afford grandma and grandpa?" in which demographer Barbara Logue is quoted as follows while speaking at the annual conference of the American Economic Association: "It's time for the U.S. to consider moving from birth control to 'death control.' . . . Death control clearly has considerable potential as a reallocative mechanism for scarce resources such as health care."

Part 13

In part 2 of my series on "Mental Health, Education and Social Control" (found in the companion to this book), I referred to Edgar C. Bundy's *Collectivism in the Church*. Bundy was general chairman of the Church League of America, and in January 1958 produced a two-part series in his periodical *News and Views* titled "Is Everybody Crazy?" Part 1 of his two-part series began with a list of statements such as the following: "If you believe that parents should teach their children right and wrong, then you are mentally ill. . . . If you believe in the great doctrines of the Christian Church as contained in the Bible, then you are mentally ill. If you prefer American Sovereignty to World Government, then you are mentally ill." Regarding these statements, Bundy said: "So say the various self-appointed guardians of the world's health, the Mental Health fanatics. . . . This group constitutes one of the most dangerous universal brain-washing brigades which has yet appeared on the scene of human activity."

Bundy then quoted from a series of lectures by psychiatrist Brock Chisholm (head of the World Health Organization), delivered in October 1945 and reprinted in *Psychiatry* (February 1946):

> For many generations we have bowed our necks to the yoke of the conviction of sin. . . . Misguided by authoritarian dogma, bound by exclusive faith, stunted by inculcated loyalty. . . . The results, the inevitable results, are frustration, inferiority, neurosis. . . . It has long been

generally accepted that parents have a perfect right to impose any points of view, any idea or fears, superstitions, prejudices, hates or faiths on their defenseless children. It is, however, only relatively recently that it has become a matter of certain knowledge that these things cause neuroses, behavior disorders, emotional disabilities, and failure to develop to a state of emotional maturity. . . . The mental health service should include provision for prophylaxis of mental disorders over the widest field. . . . Everything we think, and do and believe should be looked at. . . . We need fear no sacredness. . . .

Then Chisholm in one of the lectures says something that reads like a question that would be posed by today's New Freedom Commission on Mental Health, when he asks: "Should attempts be made by the profession to induce governments to institute compulsory treatment for the neuroses as for other infectious diseases?" At this point, we should remember Thomas Jefferson's warning from two hundred years ago when he said, "If people let government decide what foods they eat and what medicines they take, their bodies will soon be in as sorry a state as are the souls of those who live under tyranny."

Toward the end of part 1 of his two-part series, Bundy included a quote by Chisholm that appeared in the "Weekend" magazine of the *Toronto Telegram* (Vol. V, No. 10, 1955), where Chisholm declared: "A few courageous people have organized an International Planned Parenthood Association to spread the gospel of birth control. In the United States, a new foundation to deal with population problems is beginning to function with funds from the Rockefeller Foundation."

Relevant to the Rockefeller Foundation, the second part of Bundy's two-part series, "Is Everybody Crazy?", began with an announcement that the 38th annual meeting of the National Committee for Mental Hygiene (now National Association for Mental Health) was held in 1948, and was addressed by Allan Gregg of the Rockefeller Foundation. It was a two-day program and was devoted to "Preparing for World Citizenship," with the topic of the first session being "Constructing the Forces that Mold Minds." Bundy then referred to a speech by Dr. Bethuel G. Gross, Division

1 Vocational Guidance Chairman for Kiwanis in Illinois, in which Gross pronounced: "Anyone with a brain cell must recognize that the only way to prevent a child from becoming infected by the psycho-emotional cesspools of the parents is to fumigate Mom and Dad psychologically." Bundy later in part 2 referred to questions on sex relations, parental problems, etc., that were published under such titles as *Child Guidance,* which was distributed by the National Association for Mental Health.

Just prior to the two-part series by Bundy, former FBI agent Dan Smoot in *The Dan Smoot Report* (February 17, 1956) gave special attention to the subject of "Mental Health" in describing a congressional bill (H.R. 6376, passed by the U.S. House on January 18, 1956) that would authorize $12.5 million for a mental hospital and mental health program in Alaska that would make an outright gift of one million acres of the United States-owned land to the territory of Alaska. Noting that there were only about four hundred mentally ill people in Alaska at the time, Smoot suspected that there was more to this bill than met the eye, and he indicated there was a provision in the Alaska Mental Health Act whereby other states could send their mentally ill residents to Alaska. Smoot remarked, "This is the provision that has some patriotic groups calling the Alaska Mental Health Act the beginning of an American Siberia." Smoot went on to say that "throughout the Union, there is a strong, well-organized, drive for mental health legislation—most of which would permit seizure, incarceration, and treatment of 'mentally ill' people without trial by jury and without the due process of law prescribed by our Constitution."

In his report, Smoot then surmised that if the government

wanted to put someone out of the way for good, . . . government-appointed and government-paid psychiatrists could work him over. . . . They could administer treatment that would drive him insane. There are 56 different drugs which they could administer (under the pretext of treatment) which would produce amnesia and mental disorientation. There are 44 drugs which would produce delirium, associated with hallucinations, imaginary voices, and so on.

He next offered the two examples of Lucille Miller in Vermont, who protested the compulsory peacetime draft, and the Finn twins in California, who objected to governmental seizure of private property. Smoot informed that "in both cases, . . . the government finally hustled them off to distant lunatic asylums in an effort to get rid of them."

Similarly, Smoot related the case of Ron B. Ramsey, a 16-year-old high school boy in Compton, California, who wrote letters to the editor which were strongly anti-United Nations, and someone had him committed to a county institution as a mental case. Smoot then wrote that "Paul G. Hoffman's son—Halleck—diagnoses the mental illness of all who oppose the U.N. and UNESCO in these words: 'The super-patriots are clearly afraid. . . . They see a threat to the Nation in the U.N. and UNESCO,'" and Hoffman refers to them as having a paranoid delusion. But Smoot did not see these people as paranoid because, he said,

> Article 4 of the United Nations Covenant on Human Rights [states], "No one shall be subjected against his will to medical or scientific experimentation involving risk, where such is not required by his state of physical or mental health." This, of course, leaves government with unhampered "rights" to make any kind of brainwashing experiment on a citizen—if the state of his mental health requires it. It is up to government, naturally, to decide what to do about it.

For Big Brother government to identify those it deems to have "mental health problems," everyone will have to be monitored. Relevant to this, I mentioned in part 12 of this series that Congress had just passed "The REAL ID Act." U.S. Rep. David Dreier has indicated that's a good first step, but more is needed. On January 4, 2005, he introduced H.R. 98 "Illegal Immigration Enforcement and Social Security Protection Act of 2005." And on his website, one sees that this legislation would require all workers to have a Social Security card with their picture on it, and the card would "contain an electronic signature strip that contains an encrypted electronic identification strip, unique to that individual." About this, former U.S. Rep. Barry Goldwater, Jr., exclaimed: "It scares the h--- out of me. I've always been concerned about a universal ID card or system, somewhat like in Nazi Germany. That's scary. We value our privacy and freedom and are very concerned about the power of the U.S. government. A universal ID number is easy to track and record." (See "Republican David Dreier Introduces National ID Card Legislation," *Valley Morning Star*, September 27, 2004.)

Also relevant to government monitoring everyone, Audrey Hudson in "Counterterror grants fund city cameras, data mining" (*Washington Times*, May 19, 2005) reports that millions of federal dollars have been allocated to municipalities for camera surveillance systems, data-mining programs, etc., to use against terrorism. However, she quotes former Republican congressman and U.S. Attorney Bob Barr as saying about this:

> Big Brother is using his extended family as surrogates to develop and implement technology that is very invasive on privacy. This is not legitimate anti-terrorism law enforcement. It's not the responsibility of the local government to be doing this. It's naive to think the information will be kept local. Government at every level cannot seem to resist the urge to surveil and accumulate data. It's frightening what they are doing; it's truly frightening.

During the first year of President Bill Clinton's administration, Hillary Clinton's special area of concern was health, including mental health. And when George W. Bush succeeded the Clintons in the White House, it was not very long before he, too, developed his own health initiative (The New Freedom Initiative) including appointment of a New Freedom Commission on Mental Health (NFCMH). On July 22, 2003, the NFCMH recommended redesigning the mental health systems in every state, and one of the models used was the Texas Children's Medication Algorithm Project (TCMAP) rushed through in that state by then Governor George W. Bush. In an article, "Bush Texas 2-Step—TeenScreen & TMAP" (*Independent Media TV*, May 23, 2005) by investigative reporter Evelyn Pringle, one learns that TCMAP allows kids under states' care to be drugged and is still causing headaches for lawmakers today. According to an article by the Associated Press on February 9, 2005, "As lawmakers work to revampt Texas' foster care system, they also are reviewing the use of mind-altering drugs by foster children." In October 2004, the Texas inspector general for the Health and Human Services Commission said his office interviewed staff at three state licensed wilderness camps, which provide care for some foster children, and found that the average child arrives on four or five psychotropic drugs. . . . Some child advocates say that kids are being too heavily medicated once they get in the Texas foster care system. The children go into the system neurologically normal but leave neurologically damaged, Austin psychologist John Breeding said. . . . "Children are not just placed on one drug. Typically, they're placed on two or three or we've seen literally up to 17 different drugs for the same child in foster care," Breeding said. "These drugs are used as a chemical restraint." . . . The *Miami Herald* reported that one in three Florida children in state care were prescribed psychotropic drugs. . . . The files also showed that child protective service caseworkers routinely were allowed to provide consent for treatment and psychotropic drug use for children in their care, which violates Florida state law. . . . Paxil was one of the wonder drugs recommended by the TCMAP panel and was prescribed to children when the drug was new and relatively untested. . . . Lawsuits have named Paxil as the culprit in cases of murder, suicide, debilitating disease and school shootings. In June 2003, the FDA issued a warning that Paxil should not be prescribed to persons under 18 due to an alarming number of suicides by kids on this drug. In Ohio, the Medication Algorithm Project is called OMAP and just like in other states, it contains all of the most expensive psychotropic medications, and they are selling like hot cakes to children. . . . An investigation (by the *Columbus Dispatch*) found that nearly 40,000 Ohio children on Medicaid were taking drugs for anxiety, depression, delusions, hyperactivity and violent behavior as of July 2004. . . . Psychiatrists interviewed by the *Dispatch* warned that less than 25% of these drugs have been adequately tested on children. . . . There are reports that people are also being overmedicated for profit in

Pennsylvania as well. . . . Adderall is the most popular ADHD drug and
its sales in 2004 rose 28%, capturing one-fourth of the U.S. market.

Remember here that in part 12 of this series, I said that in February 2005,
Adderall was taken off the market in Canada because it was linked to twenty
sudden deaths (fourteen were children) and a dozen strokes.

Concerning the mental health screenings recommended by the NFC-
MH, most people believe that such screenings are only designed to find
people (especially children) who have serious mental health problems such
as psychosis. Therefore, most people are disinterested in the issue because
they believe it will not effect them. In the hope of alerting Americans to the
far broader applications of such screenings than most realize, the example
of what happened to a 13-year-old girl in Texas is instructive.

According to Rob Waters' "Medicating Aliah" (*Mother Jones,* May/June
2005), Aliah Gleason lived in an Austin, Texas, suburb and got in trouble
in school for running her mouth. School officials believed she had "oppositional disorder," and one day psychologists from the University of Texas
conducted a mental health screening of children at Aliah's school. About
two months later (January 2004), according to Waters,

> a child-protection worker went to Aliah's school, interviewed her, then
> summoned Calvin Gleason (Aliah's father) to the school and told him
> to take Aliah to Austin State Hospital, a state mental facility. He refused,
> and after a heated conversation, she placed Aliah in emergency custody
> and had a police officer drive her to the hospital. The Gleasons would
> not be allowed to see or even speak to their daughter for the next five
> months, and Aliah would spend a total of nine months in a state psychi-
> atric hospital and residential treatment facilities. While in the hospital,
> she was placed in restraints more than 26 times and medicated—against
> her will and without her parents' consent—with at least 12 different
> psychiatric drugs, many of them simultaneously. . . . Because Aliah lives
> in Texas, and because her commitment was involuntary, she became
> vulnerable to an even further hazard: aggressive regimens that feature
> new and controversial drugs—regimens that are promoted by drug

companies, mandated by state governments, and imposed on captive patient populations with no say over what's prescribed to them.

In a new book, *One Nation Under Therapy: How the Helping Culture Is Eroding Self-Reliance,* by Christina Hoff Sommers (former philosophy professor) and Sally Satel (psychiatrist and lecturer at the Yale School of Medicine), the authors expose the plague of "therapism," where mental health practitioners have been telling us that more than a few children and adults who are normal and well-adjusted are really mentally ill and in need of treatment.

By defining "mental health problems" in ever broader terms, the power elite will be able to include ever increasing numbers of Americans as in need of "mental health care." This will provide the power elite with grounds for limiting such people's freedom, thus enabling the power elite to mute opposition to their goal of a one-world government. The American people must resist the movement toward a one-world government and remember the admonition of Somerset Maugham: "If a nation values anything more than freedom, it will lose its freedom; and the irony of it is that if it is comfort or money that it values more, it will lose that too." In Americans' pursuit of money, they have allowed our government to make deals with Communist China that will threaten our freedom. In an article, "Magnet Consolidation Threatens Both U.S. Jobs and Security" (*In These Times,* January 23, 2004) by David Moburg, he relates that late in the summer of 2003,

> 160 high-tech magnet workers lost their jobs at Magnequench, Inc. When the seven remaining workers are laid off it will mark the end of U.S. production of the world's most advanced permanent magnets, tiny but crucial components in computers, automobiles and consumer electronic products—as well as cruise missiles and the Joint Direct Attack Munition bomb. Over the past few years Magnequench moved virtually all its U.S. production operations—and soon its headquarters and research facilities—to Mexico, Singapore and, most importantly, China. . . . Believing that government shouldn't tinker with the mar-

ket, U.S. officials surrendered a growth industry and good jobs, while making the United States dependent on China for critical military and commercial technology.

Most Americans don't realize that our government actually supported the Communist Chinese rise to power over the Nationalist Chinese in the late 1940s. Those who do know this rationalize that the Truman administration and General George Marshall simply wanted Communist China to serve as a buffer to Soviet expansion in the East much like Tito in Yugoslavia was in the Balkans. But if our leaders really didn't believe Communism was monolithic, then what was the problem with supporting Ho Chi Minh in Vietnam as a buffer to possible Communist Chinese expansion in Southeast Asia? Could it be that the real reason the Communist Chinese received our support was that the power elite wanted to bring about the exact situation we have today—unlimited cheap Chinese labor producing unlimited cheap products?

Why else do you think that even knowing Communist Chinese chairman Mao slaughtered millions of his own people, David Rockefeller could write the following in "From a China Traveller" (*New York Times,* August 10, 1973):

One is impressed immediately by the sense of national harmony. . . . There is a very real and pervasive dedication to Chairman Mao and Maoist principles. Whatever the price of the Chinese Revolution, it has obviously succeeded not only in producing more efficient and dedicated administration, but also in fostering high morale and community purpose. General social and economic progress is no less impressive. . . . The enormous social advances of China have benefitted greatly from the singleness of ideology and purpose. . . . The social experiment in China under Chairman Mao's leadership is one of the most important and successful in history.

At the time Rockefeller wrote this, he was chairman of the Council on Foreign Relations (CFR), and he was forming the Trilateral Commission (begun in 1973). More recently, you haven't heard the current President Bush refer to Communist Chinese leaders as brutal dictators (which they are) who have abused and killed (e.g., Tiananmen Square, etc.) their own people, even though he repeatedly referred to Saddam Hussein in those terms. And, of course, the American people have been co-opted into not protesting trade relations with Communist China because their 401Ks are in pension plans heavily invested in transnational corporations which are heavily invested in Communist China.

But what about the threat to our security posed by a Communist China growing in military strength because of the economic benefits we have provided them? That, too, is part of the power elite's plan for world government. Remember Study Memorandum No.7, "A World Effectively Controlled by the United Nations," written by Lincoln Bloomfield for the Institute for Defense Analysis in 1962 under contract SCC 28270 with the State Department, in which Bloomfield stated:

> A world effectively controlled by the United Nations is one in which "world government" would come about through the establishment of supranational institutions, characterized by mandatory universal membership and some ability to employ physical force. . . . [But] if the communist dynamic was greatly abated, the West might lose whatever incentive it has for world government.

Is this why Peter W. Rodman, assistant defense secretary for international security affairs in the current Bush administration, said what he did on April 14, 2005, at a joint hearing by the U.S. House International Relations and Armed Services committees? Rodman declared:

> The United States seeks a strong, prosperous and transforming China, and we support strong economic and political ties between the EU and China. Fueled by an impressive record of economic growth, China has been able to devote even greater national resources to defense modernization. This has translated into double-digit percent annual increases in Beijing's officially announced defense budget almost every year for the past 15 years.

Commenting on this attitude, William R. Hawkins in "Who wants a strong China?" (*Washington Times*, May 4, 2005) warned that "shifts in trade and investment flows are one of history's most critical factors in determining the global balance of power. It is perilous for national leaders to ignore the geopolitics of economic activity."

The effort for "A World Effectively Controlled by the United Nations" began with the planning for that organization. Leo Pasvolsky was a special assistant to the secretary of state during World War II, and he was known as the "architect" of the U.N. Charter. According to L. V. Horner (author of *The United Nations: A Threat to Our Security*) in a speech on June 17, 1963, in Oklahoma City, Pasvolsky issued a departmental memorandum regarding the objectives of his department, which were "to survey the basic principles which should underlie a desirable world order to be evolved after the termination of hostilities . . . and to devise a means of limitation of national sovereignty." One means of accomplishing Pasvolsky's goal was to create a common and receptive mindset among the people. In that regard, the UNESCO General Conference Report of 1946 revealed the following strategy:

> We are assigned the positive function of building peace in the minds of men through science, education and culture. The Executive Secretary's report gives us the blueprints for the development of what one may call a world brain, a world mind, or a world culture, which alone can be the basis of a world authority or a world government.

As usual, the U.N. has never come up with anything original on its own, and its references to a "world brain" and "world culture" probably came from the famous author H. G. Wells. In 1938, his *World Brain* was published, in which he referred to "a ruling World Brain" which would be "operating by an enhanced educational system through the whole body of mankind." Wells wrote:

> Some favour the idea of a gradual supersession of the political forms and methods of mass democracy by government through some sort of elite. . . . The general projection is in the form of a sort of modern priest-

hood, an oligarchy of professors and exceptionally competent people. Like Plato they would make the philosopher king. . . . I want to suggest something—a new social organ, a new institution—which for a time I shall call "World Encyclopaedia." . . . This World Encyclopaedia would be the mental background of every intelligent man in the world. . . . Such an Encyclopaedia would play the role of an undogmatic Bible to a world culture. . . . It would hold the world together mentally. . . . It is a super university I am thinking of, a world brain. . . . Ultimately if our dream is realized it must exert a very great influence upon everyone who controls administrations, makes wars, directs mass behaviour, feeds, moves, starves and kills populations. . . . You see how such an Encyclopaedic organization could spread like a nervous network, a system of mental control about the globe. . . . I believe that in some such way as I have sketched, the mental forces . . . could be drawn together in a real directive world intelligence.

The "world government" to which the 1946 UNESCO report referred could be a "federation of the world," about which Lord Alfred Tennyson wrote in "Locksley Hall" (Robin Hood was known as the Earl of Locksley). And the ruling "elite" to which H.G. Wells referred could have included individuals like Lord Tennyson, who was a member of the Society for Psychical Research (SPR) mentioned in part 11 of this series. Twentieth-century members of the American Society for Psychical Research included its founder William James (father of American psychology, who received his Ph.D. at Leipzig University from Wilhelm Wundt, whose grandfather was code-named "Raphael" with the Illuminati); book publisher and SPR trustee and counselor Henry Holt (James Brandt, former president of Henry Holt & Co., and G. D. Gosling, former associate editor, were both Rhodes scholars); and anthropologist Margaret Mead (whose husband Gregory Bateson led the CIA's MK-Ultra project). Mead's father-in-law, William Bateson, was a member of the SPR. And Mead's daughter, Mary Catherine Bateson, accompanied New Ager and SPR member Jean Houston to Camp David, and they helped Hillary Clinton write *It Takes a Village*.

To combat the power elite's plan for a one-world government, Americans should promote patriotism and respect for our flag beginning at an early age. One way to foster this is to contact the National Flag Foundation (one of the foremost leaders in patriotic education) at *flag@americanflags. org* (or call 1-800-615-1776) and ask for information on "Flag Facts" and "Young Patriots Education Initiatives" (more than four thousand schools have asked the foundation to find sponsors for them for the Young Patriots program).

Before it is too late, we should heed the advice of our second U.S. president, John Adams. For the fiftieth anniversary of the Declaration of Independence, the 91-year-old founding father Adams offered his final public toast: "Independence forever." And if he were alive today, he might add: "World government never." Americans should also remember the warning of Adams' son (and future president) John Quincy Adams, when as U.S. secretary of state he addressed the U.S. House of Representatives on July 4, 1821, and pronounced:

> America goes not abroad in search of monsters to destroy. She is the well-wisher to the freedom and independence of all. She is the champion and vindicator only of her own. She will commend the general cause by the countenance of her voice, and the benignant sympathy of her example. She well knows that by once enlisting under other banners than her own, were they even the banners of foreign independence, she would involve herself beyond the power of extrication in all the wars of interest and intrigue, of individual avarice, envy and ambition, which assume the colors and usurp the standard of freedom. The fundamental maxims of her policy would insensibly change from liberty to force.

America today is not heeding John Quincy Adams' warning.

Part 14

In part 13 of this series, I briefly mentioned the new book, *One Nation Under Therapy: How the Helping Culture Is Eroding Self-Reliance* (2005), by Christina Hoff Sommers and Sally Satel, M.D. The authors claim that

> children, more than any group, are targeted for therapeutic improvement.
> . . . The propensity of experts to pathologize and medicalize healthy children en masse has gotten way out of hand. The past decade has seen a cascade of books and articles promoting the idea that seemingly content and well-adjusted Americans—adults as well as children—are emotionally damaged.

Unfortunately, President George W. Bush's New Freedom Commission on Mental Health (NFCMH) has proposed screening all of America's youth. Used to support this initiative will be the recent findings of the National Comorbidity Survey Replication (NCSR), the results of which are published in the June edition of the *Archives of General Psychiatry*. It found that half of those who will ever be diagnosed with a mental disorder show signs of the disease by age fourteen. In Rick Weiss' "Study: U.S. Leads In Mental Illness, Lags in Treatment" (*Washington Post*, June 7, 2005), one also learns that the National Institute of Mental Health (NIMH) funded the $20 million NCSR study, which found that one-quarter of all Americans met the criteria for having a mental illness within the past year. The study also found that almost half of Americans meet the criteria for such an illness at some point in their lives, and that less than half of those in need get treated. Thomas Insel, chief of the NIMH, expressed his disappointment to learn from the survey that about a third of people in need rely solely on nonprofessional sources such as internet support groups and spiritual advisers. You might ask yourself at this point what kind of broad definition they are using to determine that half of the American population will be mentally ill at some point, and you might also ask what is wrong with relying upon spiritual advisers?

Countering advocates of mental health screening, Dr. Karen Effrem in an October 31, 2004, letter to the *Washington Times* titled "Go Slow on Mental Health Screening" cautioned:

> Given the very real problems of already existing coercion, subjective criteria, dangerous and ineffective medication, and the failure of screening to prevent suicide, none of which are covered in the NFC report, Congress would be wise to withhold the $44 million requested for state grants to implement the NFC recommendations. Whatever good may come from the other recommendations is completely overshadowed by the loss of freedom and damage that would come from labeling and drugging potentially millions of children based on these unsupportable screening and treatment programs. If we don't act now, every child in America will be screened for mental illness: thousands, perhaps millions, will be deemed "at risk" of developing mental health problems for which they will be prescribed powerful psychotropic drugs. The screening plan has been called Orwellian and diabolical—the treatment "model" the report recommends is a drug-industry sponsored guideline—the Texas Medication Algorithm Project (TMAP).

The first TMAP model was adopted in 1995 in Texas when President Bush was governor of that state.

One of the major forces behind TMAP was the Robert Wood Johnson Foundation (RWJF) mentioned in earlier parts of this series. About the time TMAP began in 1995, the RWJF gave a sizeable grant for TMAP to

Dr. Ken Altshuler in the psychiatry department at the University of Texas and Dr. John Rush in pharmacology at the same university. Chairman of the RWJF's National Advisory Council for its Mental Health Services Program for Youth (MHSPY) was former North Carolina governor James B. Hunt, Jr. After the foundation's MHSPY National Program Office in 1990 awarded implementation grants to eight states, it then awarded replication grants to eleven states, including Texas, between July 1994 and October 1996. In Texas and other states, the Child and Adolescent Strengths Assessment (CASA) was used, looking at whether a child had a particular vocational skill, an ability to trust others, and experienced religious/spiritual beliefs among other things. The states used outcomes-based planning and implemented outcomes-based systems of care.

The TMAP, of course, was not the first government program regarding children's mental health. On September 29, 1970, a Special Studies Subcommittee (U.S. Rep. Cornelius Gallagher, presiding chairman) of the Committee on Government Operations held hearings on "Federal Involvement in the Use of Behavior Modification Drugs on Grammar School Children of the Right to Privacy Inquiry." At the beginning of the hearings, Rep. Gallagher stated:

> I want to welcome you here today to our hearing into Federal responsibility in promoting the use of amphetamines (e.g., Dexedrine and Ritalin) to modify the behavior of grammar school children. . . . From the time of puberty onward, each and every child is told that "speed kills" and that amphetamines are to be avoided. Yet, this same child has learned that Ritalin, for example, is the only thing which makes him a functioning member of the school environment and both his family and his doctor have urged the pills on him. I am frankly very curious about the kind of credibility his parents have when they try to guide him away from amphetamines after encouraging him to take them.

He concluded his introductory remarks by listing a number of 1970 NIMH grants, among which were R01 MH 18180 for $102,076 to test the full range of FDA-approved psychotropic drugs for their effects on children, to establish guidelines for safe and effective use of psychotropic drugs in the treatment of emotional disorders in the young. And he listed R01 MH 18579 for $60,185 to evaluate the relative efficacy of thioridazine, methylphenidate (Ritalin), thioridazine-methylphenidate combination, and placebo in hyperkinetic children between ages 6 and 12.

Following the list, Dr. Ronald Lipman, chief of the clinical studies section of the NIMH, testified that "after the age of 12 these drugs (amphetamines) should be given with extreme caution, if at all." He later indicated that "the estimates we have are from 3 to 10 percent of those up to 12 years of age" have MBD (minimal brain dysfunction). This was succeeded by a prepared statement by Theodore Johnson, a chemist with the Veterans' Administration, who observed that

> the most grotesque of proposals reached President Nixon, December 1969, by memorandum from Dr. Arnold Hutschnecker, a psychiatrist and consultant to the National Commission on the Causes and Prevention of Violence. He suggested that all 6- to 8-year-old U.S. children be required to take psychological tests to determine whether they had a predeliction for criminal behavior, and to weed out the potentially dangerous. This program would have been implemented by the construction of "rehabilitation camps," day-care centers and after school centers, where the children could be treated. I have been informed that Dr. Hutschnecker was educated in Berlin, Germany, in 1939. This may explain the insight he shared with the President. "There are Pavlovian methods which I have seen effectively used in the Soviet Union." Perhaps even more alarming, is the fact that the President sent this ludicrous thing to HEW for advice on setting up pilot projects.

Chairman Gallagher next challenged Dr. John Peters (with the Child Study Center at the University of Arkansas Medical Center), who had been using Imipramine in a study by reading from the Tofranil (which is included in Imipramine and hydrochloride) warning label, which states: "Pending evaluation of results from clinical trials in children, the drug is not recommended for use to patients under 12 years of age. We don't have information that has been systematically studied in hyperkinetic behavior for these children."

Included at the conclusion of the hearings was John Mathews' article, "Set Up Data Banks, Allen Urges Schools" (*Washington Star,* April 15, 1970), which began:

> U.S. Commissioner of Education James E. Allen, Jr. has outlined a plan for restructuring local schools that would include computerized data systems designed to help professionals "prescribe" programs for helping pupils and their families. . . . In his proposal, made yesterday in a speech to the National School Boards Association convention in San Francisco, Allen suggested each local school system should have a central diagnostic center "to find out everything possible about the child and his background" to plan an individualized program for him. After test and home visits, Allen said, the center "would know just about everything there is to know about the child—his home and family background, his cultural and language deficiencies, his health and nutrition needs and his general potential as an individual." The information would be fed into a computer for use by a team of trained professionals who would write a "prescription" for the child "and if necessary, for his home and family as well," Allen said. "If the home is contributing negatively to the child's development, it too should receive attention and aid."

There are powerful forces working toward the destruction of the traditional family as well as the souls of our children and our grandchildren. Some years ago, the British Humanist Association published a discussion document, "Marriage and the Family," in which one reads that "some opponents of Humanism have accused us of wishing to overthrow the traditional Christian family. They are right. That is exactly what we intend to do."

One way the traditional Christian family is being undermined is by what is taught in our schools. The National Education Association (NEA) has a Gay and Lesbian Caucus, and at an NEA annual convention, lesbians promoted a ninety-minute video titled "It's Elementary: Teaching About Gay Issues at Schools." Also, the American Library Association produced a list of "Gay Materials for Use in Schools" as long ago as 1978.

Another way our traditional Christian families are being undermined is via values clarification. Earlier in this series, I explained how this process has been used in government schools. As nationally syndicated columnist Thomas Sowell wrote in "Schools brainwash vulnerable kids" (*West County Times*, September 28, 1990):

> There is a whole spectrum of courses and programs designed to brainwash children into rejecting the values, beliefs and ways of life taught them by the parents—and to accept the latest fad thinking on subjects ranging from death to sex to social philosophies in general. Whatever the particular subject matter, these programs follow standard brainwashing techniques of putting the victims under emotional stress, breaking down their inhibitions and destroying their links to others on the outside. With schoolchildren, the link that must be loosened or broken is the child's link to his or her parents. In innumerable ways, some very subtle, these programs undermine, ridicule, or otherwise sidetrack parents as irrelevant.

Values clarification has also been used outside of schools. For example, in the late 1970s, under a contract with the U.S. Army, humanist Sidney Simon implemented a values clarification program which the contract said "is an experimental program to change attitudes and behavior of 12,000 soldiers. . . ." Concerning this, U.S. Senator Strom Thurmond on December 12, 1979, wrote a letter to the deputy secretary of defense, saying:

> . . . Obviously the use of this type of course in the Army raises many questions. It is a form of psychotherapy. The questions are predetermined and the choices preselected. Thus the narrow options given the student are actually a subtle form of political or philosophical indoctrination. . . . Many also see this type of course as an attack on the family when Simon says in his book *Values Clarification* that "young people brought up by moralizing adults are not prepared to make their own responsible choices." There is a strong implication that family and church guid-

ance have left the individual unable to cope with the modern world. . . . Mr. Secretary, in my view government has no right to modify the behavior of soldiers through a humanistic program of this type. . . . I consider efforts to open the military to this type of program a dangerous precedent. . . .

In addition, moral absolutes are under attack by the popular culture. For example, the most recent Star Wars film, *Revenge of the Sith,* in which the Sith are the villains, contains a statement by hero Obi-wan Kenobi that "only the Sith speak in absolutes." The clear implication is that those who believe in moral absolutes are villains.

We cannot stand idly by as the principles of our Judeo-Christian religion are being undermined. Often today this undermining comes in the form of a watered-down gospel rather than a direct challenge. It's as though Richard Gardner's infamous April 1974 *Foreign Affairs* article were retitled "The Hard Road to a New World Religion" and as if his message were paraphrased to say "an end run around the gospel, eroding it piece-by-piece, will get us further [to a new world religion] than the old-fashioned frontal assault." We should heed the words of Bishop James Madison (second cousin of President Madison) in his sermon, "Manifestations of the Beneficence of Divine Providence Towards America," preached in Richmond, Virginia, on February 19, 1795 (proclaimed a day of thanksgiving and prayer by President Washington), when he said:

> The moment that religion, the pure and undefiled religion, which heaven, in compassion to the infirmity of human reason, vouchsafed to mortals, loses its influence over their hearts, from that fatal moment, farewell to public and private happiness, farewell, a long farewell to virtue, to patriotism, to liberty!

We cannot let the plans of the power elite succeed. "Therefore let us not sleep, as others do, but let us watch . . ." (1 Thess. 5:6). We must join in this war for hearts, minds, and souls. We must keep informed, inform others, and "pray without ceasing" (1 Thess. 5:17).

Part 15

Concerning the New Freedom Commission on Mental Health's (NFCMH) recommendation that all American youth receive mental health screenings, after thoughtful prayer to God for guidance, we must take action to oppose the enforcement of any such screenings. First, we should question the federal Department of Education's current expenditure of $5 million on "Mental Health Integration in Schools" and U.S. Senator Edward Kennedy's "Foundations for Learning" mental health program at a cost of $1 million. Secondly, we should oppose the congressional H.R. 2123 "School Readiness Act of 2005" (also known as the Head Start Reauthorization Bill) introduced May 5, 2005, with its (Rep. Tom) Osborne Amendment (passed May 18 in committee) because among other things, four times it inserts language covering "mental and behavioral health services."

Thirdly, we should support U.S. Rep. John Kline's "Child Medication Safety Act" (H.R. 1790) introduced in Congress on April 21, 2005, with sixteen co-sponsors to prohibit schools from coercing parents into having their children placed on psychotropic drugs in order to attend school. Knight-Ridder nationally syndicated psychologist John Rosemond in "Normal becomes 'disabled'" (*News And Observer,* May 14, 2002) commented:

> I say educators and mental health professionals are analyzing kids to death. They are also diagnosing and labeling children to death, and

medicating children to death. This will, in fact, eventually be the Death of Childhood in America. In time, every child strays significantly from some norm. Slowly but surely, the medical and psychological industries are turning every such instance of strain into a diagnosis, thus creating a huge client pool in perpetuity. The truly sad thing is that most American parents are cooperating in this travesty.

Fourthly, we should object to mandatory mental health screening of our children by citing the Protection of Pupil Rights Amendment (PPRA), also called the Hatch Amendment (Public Law 95-561, Section 1250, passed November 1, 1978), which states that

> No student shall be required, as part of any applicable program, to submit to psychiatric examination, testing, or treatment, or psychological examination, testing, or treatment, in which the primary purpose is to reveal information concerning: . . . mental and psychological problems potentially embarrassing to the student or his family. . . .

In an April 12, 2005, letter from the Family Policy Compliance Office of the U. S. Department of Education, it indicated that the PPRA applies to surveys even when they are not funded by the U.S. Department of Education. It further stated: "PPRA applies to local educational agencies [school districts] that are the recipients of any funds from the Department of Education. So, in essence, a public school giving a survey funded by HHS or by the Lions Club would have to comply with PPRA."

And more recently than the PPRA, we can cite the Tiahrt Amendment (H.R. 3189, 105th Congress, 1998), which amended Section 444 of the General Education Provisions Act (20 U.S.C. 1232g) and stated:

> No funds shall be made available under any applicable program to an educational agency or institution that, as part of an applicable program and without the prior, written, informed consent of the parent of a student, requires the student—(1) to undergo medical, psychological, or psychiatric examination, testing, treatment, or immunization (except

in the case of a medical emergency); or (2) to reveal any information about the student's personal or family life [except to the extent necessary to comply with the Child Abuse Prevention and Treatment Act (42 U.S.C. 5102)].

The Tiahrt Amendment was attached to the "No Child Left Behind Act of 2001" (Public Law 107-110, signed January 8, 2002), which also amended Section 445(b) of the General Education Provisions Act regarding student privacy to disallow asking students about "mental or psychological problems of the student or the student's family, . . . or the religious practices, affiliations, or beliefs of the student or student's parent . . . [without] prior written parental consent." And according to the May 2003 edition of *Health and Health Care in Schools,* these prohibitions apply "even when the surveys are not Education Department-funded."

One cautionary note, however, is in order regarding the PPRA and Tiahrt Amendment. While both are good and useful, Rep. Ron Paul's H.R. 181 "The Parental Consent Act of 2005" (which now has forty-four co-sponsors) is still needed because there are "exceptions" under PPRA and the Tiahrt Amendment. Under the Tiahrt Amendment, for example, "testing material" does not include a non-classroom diagnostic test or a test subject to a copyright agreement. Unfortunately, this is a hole through which mental health screeners could drive an invasive "diagnostic" truck!

Rep. Paul's legislation is also needed because children are already being screened without parental consent. According to Rhonda Robinson's report on June 10, 2005, in the *Illinois Leader,* the Rutherford Institute has filed a tort claim against Penn High School and administrators in Mishawaka, Indiana, who conducted the TeenScreen survey on Michael and Teresa Rhoades' 15-year-old daughter without their permission. Robinson related that

> personnel of the Madison Center for Children, a division of the community mental health center in St. Joseph County, Indiana, administered the TeenScreen mental health examination. The Rhoades became aware of the screening only when their daughter came home and asked what

was the definition of obsessive-compulsive disorder and social anxiety disorder. She explained that was the diagnosis she had been given at school after the survey.

Furthermore, Capitol Resource Institute in a press release June 16, 2005, indicated that

> by a four-to-one vote, the Nevada County (California) Joint Union High School District (NJUHSD) voted Wednesday [June 15] to uphold a district policy to restrict parents' knowledge concerning their children's absence from campus. Claiming that children as young as age 12 should be emancipated from their parents when it comes to certain medical and psychological services, . . . rights activists proposed that the district maintain a policy of not notifying parents when students leave campus for these appointments. . . . Dan Miller, NJUHSD board chairman, prefaced his vote against parents by stating that school teachers are "surrogate parents."

Rep. Paul attempted to get a shorthand version of his legislation attached to a Labor, Health and Human Services, and Education Appropriations bill (H.R. 3010), but on June 24, 2005, his amendment was defeated 304–97 in the U.S. House of Representatives. All his amendment said was that "none of the funds made available in this Act may be used to create or implement any new universal mental health screening program." In his June 27, 2005, newsletter, "Federal Funding for Mental Health Screening of Kids," Rep. Paul wrote: "On Friday [June 24] Congress defeated an amendment I introduced that would have prevented the federal government from moving forward with an Orwellian program to mandate mental health screening of kids in schools." H.R. 3010 passed with $26 million for "state incentive transformation grants" to fund the New Freedom Commission on Mental Health (NFCMH) recommendations. While the NFCMH recommendations do not say the screening is "mandatory," they also do not say it is "voluntary." Rather, they say the screening should be "universal," and Rep. Paul asks: "How can you have something universal if you are not going to be testing everybody?" My own question to those who opposed Rep. Paul's amendment is "Even if you believe his amendment was unnecessary because the legislation does not 'mandate' screening everyone, what would it have hurt to vote for his amendment just in case some bureaucrat wanted to write regulations interpreting universal mental health screening as requiring everyone's participation?"

Concerning TeenScreen mentioned above, in May 2004, the Illinois legislature passed a resolution approving the implementation of TeenScreen in public schools. TeenScreen is supposed to be a suicide-prevention program, but several years after its introduction into Tulsa, Oklahoma, schools, the suicide rate rose dramatically.

TeenScreen has been recommended by the New Freedom Commission on Mental Health (NFCMH), which also recommended the Texas Medication Algorithm Project (TMAP) drug treatment program. According to Evelyn Pringle's "TeenScreen Sets Up Shop In Illinois" (*Independent Media TV*, June 19, 2005), TMAP "specifically requires doctors to prescribe the newer generation of psychiatric drugs to children, including the antidepressants known as Selective Serotonin Reuptake Inhibitors (SSRIs) that can lead children to commit suicide or other violent acts." SSRIs impair serotonin metabolism, and Pringle relates that "in one study reviewed by the FDA panel, in a pool of 931 depressed patients taking SSRIs listed on the TMAP, versus 811 depressed patients taking a placebo, there were 52 suicidal acts by people on the SSRIs versus 18 on placebo."

IMAP (the Illinois version of TMAP) is in at least twenty-three Illinois counties, and its drug list is the same as TMAP's. According to the plan for Illinois, in addition to children, all pregnant women are to be screened for depression up to one year following their babies' births. Pringle indicates that "the treatment for depression mandated by the IMAP drug list will be the SSRI antidepressants even though new studies indicate that SSRIs taken by pregnant women can have serious adverse affects on the unborn fetus."

The Illinois Children's Mental Health Act of 2003 was passed largely due to a report by the Illinois Children's Mental Health Task Force, which was in part funded by the Robert Wood Johnson Foundation mentioned earlier in this series. The task force's final report was released in April 2003, and according to Evelyn Pringle, it called for

> a comprehensive, coordinated children's mental health system comprised of prevention, early intervention, and treatment for children ages 0-18 years and for a statewide data-reporting system to track information on each person, and social-emotional development screens with all mandated school exams (K, 4th, and 9th).

The Illinois Children's Mental Health Act created the Illinois Children's Mental Health Partnership, which is supposed to develop a final plan by June 30, 2005. Although the current draft of the Partnership's plan contains the words, "voluntary" and "parental consent," it's an opt-out provision and there is no mention of parental notification. This raises the obvious question: "How are parents supposed to opt their children out of a mental health screening they have not been informed will take place?"

There is a tremendous amount of money driving this effort, as the Illinois plan stresses that treatment should be funded by Medicaid. And Illinois is not alone in this regard, as in Evelyn Pringle's article mentioned above, one reads:

> On January 15, 2005, the *Miami Herald* reported that nearly 1,900 children under the care of Florida's child welfare system are taking anti-depressant drugs, despite a strong federal warning that such medications are linked to an increased risk of suicidal thinking. Similar findings held true in Tennessee for kids covered by the State insurance program. A study conducted in 2004 by Dr. William Cooper, an associate professor of pediatrics at Vanderbilt University in Nashville, determined that the use of antipsychotic drugs among low-income children in Tennessee had nearly doubled between 1996 and 2001. Cooper's report, published in the August 3, 2004, issue of the *Archives of Pediatric Adolescent Medicine*, found that young people who are not psychotic are being prescribed anti-psychotic drugs for which there was no data on safety or effectiveness.

A brief note of encouragement is in order here. Thanks to the efforts of Texas Eagle Forum and others, an amendment (implementing aspects of the NFCMH recommendations) to H.B.2572 (mental health/mental retardation reform legislation) was withdrawn from the Texas legislature in late May 2005 before adjournment. In addition, Georgia state senator Nancy Schaefer has authored a resolution, SR 128, opposing the mental health screening of children. At a May 22, 2005, Atlanta, Georgia, rally against mental health screening, Senator Schaefer said, "Children belong to parents. . . . Children and families are under dangerous assault today!" She is correct. Unfortunately, former Arizona state superintendent of education Carolyn Warner has declared that "those who educate are more to be honored than those who bear the children. The latter gave them only life, the former teach them the art of living." Senator Schaefer further remarked:

> Parents are coerced to put their children on psychotropic medications and children are dying from it. . . . Behavior programs such as outcome-based education, values clarification, mastery learning, psychological and psychiatric questionnaires, and self-esteem are nothing more than a psychologically controlled environment to induce certain beliefs or politically correct thinking. . . . Stand up, speak out, and get involved. If you don't, you empower the enemy. . . . The time is now. If we miss this opportunity, we will lose a generation.

I have mentioned above the "No Child Left Behind Act of 2001" (NCLB), and it is useful here to see how this is part of the dialectical process. NCLB applies primarily to education before the high school level, but with the graduation rate of American students seventeenth among developed nations, President Bush has announced that he wants NCLB applied to high schools as well. Responding to this call, Michael Cohen (president of ACHIEVE) released a report of The American Diploma Project, a partnership of the Education Trust, Thomas B. Fordham Foundation, and ACHIEVE. The report is called "Creating a High School Diploma That Counts."

What has all this got to do with the dialectical process which the power elite employs? Cohen was a liberal holdover from the Carter administration who wrote "Goals 2000" for President Clinton, and ACHIEVE was designed to promote American students meeting national and international education standards. ACHIEVE's first president was Robert Schwartz (formerly director of the education grant-making program of the Pew Charitable Trusts) who is on the board of the Education Trust, established by the American Association of Higher Education and funded by liberal groups such as the Pew Charitable Trusts, John D. and Catherine T. Mac-Arthur Foundation, Annie E. Casey Foundation, Carnegie Corporation of New York, and the Bill and Melinda Gates Foundation. Cohen worked just down the hall from me at the U.S. Department of Education, where my boss was Chester Finn (appointed by Secretary of Education William J. Bennett under President Reagan), who now heads the Thomas B. Fordham Foundation (a member of the U.S. National Commission for UNESCO) and who wants a national curriculum.

Internationalizing education has long been part of the power elite's plan to prepare people for world government. On the occasion of the bicentennial of the Declaration of Independence, a Declaration of Interdependence was written by Henry Steele Commager stating: "We must join with others to bring forth a new world order." The document also decried "narrow notions of national sovereignty" and called for strengthening the United Nations and broadening the jurisdiction of the World Court. Helen Wise, chairman of the National Education Association's (NEA) Bicentennial Committee, was on the advisory committee to draft the document, and those involved "worked to ensure that its precepts would be included in the curricula and texts of our schools."

Also on the advisory committee were Rhodes Scholars Harlan Cleveland and Richard Gardner. Gardner had written about "eroding national sovereignty piece by piece" in the Council on Foreign Relations' *Foreign Affairs* (April 1974). Cleveland headed the Aspen Institute for Humanistic Studies' Program in International Affairs, and the Institute organized a National Commission on Coping with Interdependence which, in partnership with the Rockefeller and Kettering Foundations (and acting on a suggestion by the State Department), assessed Americans' willingness to change their thinking and ways to accept global interdependence. This seemed to follow the philosophy expressed by Lord Bertrand Russell in his 1959 address to "The Future of Man" symposium sponsored by Joseph E. Seagram & Sons, Inc., on the dedication of its New York City headquarters. Russell admonished that "you've got to get international feeling into the world if the human race is to survive. . . . The only way that I can see in which a scientific society can become stable and survive for long periods is the establishment of one single World Authority possessing all the serious weapons of war."

Facilitating Americans' acceptance of "global interdependence" have been recent actions by a majority of the members of the U.S. Supreme Court. For example, when the supposedly conservative Justice Sandra Day O'Connor dedicated Georgetown University's new international law center on October 26, 2004, she pronounced that international law "is vital if judges are to faithfully discharge their duties. We operate today under a very large array of international agreements, treaties, organizations." Also in 2004, for the first time in history, the Supreme Court allowed a foreign entity (the Commission of the European Communities) to present oral arguments as a "friend of the Court."

Most recently, the allegedly conservative Justice O'Connor provided the deciding margin in the Supreme Court's June 27, 2005, five to four attack upon the Jewish and Christian religions by outlawing Kentucky's courthouses' display of the Ten Commandments. Justice Antonin Scalia opposed the ruling, referring to "the dictatorship of a shifting Supreme Court majority."

Writing for the majority, Justice David Souter expressed the need for "government neutrality between religion and religion, and between religion and nonreligion." But this is sheer hypocrisy, because while they ban the Ten Commandments, they have not banned the pagan goddess Themis (blindfolded with scales in hand) from courthouses across the land. This double standard by the Supreme Court actually could be considered anti-Semitism, because God gave the Ten Commandments to Moses, a leader of the Jewish people. This discrimination by the Supreme Court must cease, and so should any other displays of pagan deities on public property, often there at public expense.

It is my hope that this series will inspire people to keep informed and then take appropriate action when needed to restore biblical morality and traditional education, and to preserve the traditional family, the principles upon which America was founded (included the right to reject mental health screenings as an invasion of privacy), and our national sovereignty—for the sake of America's future. Relevant to this, there was a Freedom 21 National Conference July 14–16, 2005, in Reno, Nevada. For more information on the conference, see *www.freedom21.org.*

PRAY FOR AMERICA!!

About the Author

Dennis Laurence Cuddy, historian and political analyst, received a Ph.D. from the University of North Carolina at Chapel Hill (major in American history, minor in political science). Dr. Cuddy has taught at the university level, has been a political and economic risk analyst for an international consulting firm, and has been a senior associate with the U.S. Department of Education.

Cuddy has also testified before members of Congress on behalf of the U.S. Department of Justice. Dr. Cuddy has authored or edited twenty-one books and booklets, and has written hundreds of articles appearing in newspapers around the nation, including the *Washington Post, Los Angeles Times,* and *USA Today.* He has been a guest on numerous radio talk shows in various parts of the country, such as ABC Radio in New York City, and he has also been a guest on the national television programs USA Today and CBS's Nightwatch.